The Bible and the American Myth
A Symposium on the Bible and Constructions of Meaning

D0898369

<u>Cover.</u> *Daniel Interpreting the Writing on the Wall.* From a 19th-century engraving by A. D. Ligny of a drawing by Gustave Doré (1832–1883). "Immediately the fingers of a human hand appeared and began writing on the plaster of the wall of the royal palace, next to the lampstand. . . . And this is the writing that was inscribed: MENE, MENE, TEKEL, and PARSIN. This is the interpretation of the matter: MENE, God has numbered the days of your kingdom and brought it to an end; TELEL, you have been weighed on the scales and found wanting; PERES, your kingdom is divided and given to the Medes and Persians." (Daniel 5:5, 25-28 NRSV)

• Studies in American Biblical Hermeneutics 16 •

The Bible and the American Myth

A Symposium on the Bible and Constructions of Meaning

edited by
Vincent L. Wimbush

MERCER UNIVERSITY PRESS

1979 • 1999

TWENTY YEARS OF PUBLISHING EXCELLENCE

ISBN 0-86554-650-9   MUP/P193

The Bible and the American Myth.
A Symposium on the Bible and Constructions of Meaning.
Copyright ©1999
Mercer University Press, Macon, Georgia 31210-3960 USA
All rights reserved
Exceptions: see previous copyright notices on p. x, below
Printed in the United States of America

The paper used in this publication meets
the minimum requirements of American National Standard
for Information Sciences—Permanence of Paper
for Printed Library Materials, ANSI Z39.48-1984.

Library of Congress Cataloging-in-Publication Data

The Bible and the American myth :
a symposium on the Bible and constructions of meaning /
edited by Vincent L. Wimbush.
x+190pp. 6x9" (15x23cm.) —
(Studies in American biblical hermeneutics ; 16)
Includes bibliographical references and indexes.
ISBN 0-86554-650-9 (alk. paper).
1. Bible—Influence—Congresses.
2. Bible—Use—Congresses.
3. United States—Civilization—Congresses.
I. Wimbush, Vincent L.   II. Series.
BS538.7.B543   1999
220'.0973—dc21   99-14470   **CIP**

Contents

Series Editor's Preface

The American myth stands alone as the preeminent issue of American biblical hermeneutics. The peculiar aspect of the American myth is that it is really not American at all, but European in its original conception. It first achieved the power to define a culture among the founding fathers of New England, where it bubbled to the surface of human consciousness through the intellectual tools brought to God's New Israel from old England. The persistence of the myth from the venerable Massachusetts Bay Colony through our own Vietnamesque landscape is a symbol of the power of borrowed intellectual ideas, and the failure of intellectual nerve which tenaciously clings to the brief moments of life that God grants each of us. Its persistence as a silent presence in "America's most segregated hour" of Sunday morning worship is readily visible in the myriad of American flags across the land that adorn our worship of the God who created all human beings, indeed all living beings.

In the briefest way possible, I will suggest what I take to be important aspects of the American myth as a preface to this provocative little volume. In this regard, the broadest general truth is that the problem of reading the Bible within the American cultural context stands as a significant instance of the general problem of the relationship between religion and culture. Religion is the child of religion—born within culture, nurtured by culture, even as all the while it seeks to transform culture. Religion and culture are powerful bedfellows, and stand in especially dangerous symbiotic relationship for the welfare of all when that power is ignored or denied, and the borders between them become transparent.

Secondly, it is crucial for Americans to recognize the peculiarity which the American setting brings to our reading of the Bible. It is our national text—whether we really read it or not. It is axiomatic that Americans, when confronted with the raw ideas of the Declaration of Independence, find much of it overly radical and subversive to their well-being and happiness. Little of that radical (prophetic) power stills exists in the common understanding of the Bible. The passages we commonly refer to, or recall from childhood memory, delineate a God of love and forgiveness, and eventually in adulthood, a God of wealth and prosperity. But, at least we care enough about the Bible to distort it and interpret it out of this hermeneutics of privilege. Imperceptibly, all of us seem to be learning to accommodate that benign neglect in our time.

The same cannot be said for our poor little Declaration of Independence. That is a text that we by and large leave for our newly arrived immigrants to learn, in order to pass the necessary exams, to receive the necessary papers of legitimization and documentation. The Bible, on the other hand, we must interpret and live as if we do not live in woeful ignorance of it. We Americans apparently don't want to eliminate our heritage—whether it be religious, educational, governmental, or the like. It is a far better strategy to dumb down that heritage as we rush headlong into the brave new world of the transformation of the Jeffersonian pursuit of happiness into entertainment.

Thirdly, the problem which this collection of essays addresses is rooted in the fact that no other society in the world is so imbued both with the aura and aroma of the Bible, while simultaneously subjecting it to such parasitic cultural captivity. The symbiosis of the Bible and the American myth of exceptionality and mission mirrors the symbiosis of an unhealthy relationship between the child and mother. And, just as until that symbiotic bond is broken in the individual human interactive process neither the mother nor the child are free to become children of God, the same may be said at the societal level for the liberating power of the Bible, and the true calling of America among the nations. We must come to recognize that to speak of the American national self-interest, and America as a Christian nation, are mutually exclusive terms. We must come to recognize that the Balkanization of American life into urban/suburban, black/white, rich/poor, elite/subservient classes, and similar polarities that abound among us, excludes the American way of life from any reasonable pretense of Christian identity. Somewhere the church must find the courage to proclaim loudly and clearly, that America's wars are precisely that, America's wars, not God's.

This little book reflects the power of what can happen when bright, passionate minds embrace the problem of the American myth. I rejoice in what Vincent Wimbush has fashioned and brought about here. No other American biblical scholar until now has responded more courageously to the issue of deconstructing the American myth. That Vincent is African-American may or may not be of significant relevance to this fact and the text before you. I do not know. More importantly, I believe that question is ultimately irrelevant.

What finally matters is that a theologian finally loves the Bible enough, and finally loves his culture enough, to question how both are being used in our time and place for the gain of the few, at the expense of the many.

Thank you, Vincent, for your vision—and the vision of those you have gathered to take seriously the largely ignored prophetic voice of the Bible.

4 April 1999   *Charles Mabee*
Ecumenical Theological Seminary, Detroit

Acknowledgments

The photos on p. 37 are from *Indian Life. News from Across Native North America* 17/1 (March–April 1996): 9, by permission of the publisher, Intertribal Christian Communications Inc., Winnipeg, Manitoba. Cutlines: (top) "The Band of Six: Native American Pastors set out on a 168-mile walk to Atlanta, declaring 'No More Broken Treaties.' They are (L to R) Daron Butler, Jon Lansa, Craig Smith, Huron Claus, Tom Claus, and Leon Matthews"; (bottom) "There was a real moving of the Holy Spirit during the '96 Promise Keepers Clergy Conference attended by 47,000 pastors from all denominations and cultural backgrounds. Six hundred Native American pastors were there."

The image on p. 57 depicting an Audio-Animatronics® figure of Abraham Lincoln is from the *Great Moments with Mr. Lincoln* attraction at DisneyLand® Park, copyright ©Disney Enterprises, Inc., by arrangement with the Disney Publishing Group.

The drawing on p. 72 of "Dr. Briggs in His Study at Home" is from a booklet published by Union Theological Seminary, by courtesy of the Burke Library of Union Theological Seminary in the City of New York: *Charles Augustus Briggs, Union Theological Seminary, and 20th Century American Protestantism*, Burke Library Occasional Publication no. 2 (1994). The original illustration by H. T. Smith was reproduced in the booklet from clippings from the *New York World* (1891) in the Burke Library Archives.

The "Heaven's Gate" home-page logo on p. 158 is from the mirror site http://www.heavensgatetoo.com and is reproduced by permission of the Telah Foundation, Phoenix, Arizona.

Introduction

And the Students
Shall Teach Them . . .

The Study of the Bible and the Study
of Meaning Construction

Vincent L. Wimbush

The essays that constitute this collection were originally written as part of the requirements of an advanced seminar on the Bible and the (De)Construction of the American Myth, directed by me and held at Union Theological Seminary, New York City, during the fall semester 1997. The seminar was designed to challenge students to think about the Bible not so much in terms of ancient historical events and cultures or in terms of ancient culture-specific texts, their literary and rhetorical forms—the preoccupations, even fetishes, of modern traditional academic biblical studies—but in terms of the influence of the Bible in the construction and legitimation, deconstruction, and delegitimation of the world that we all know, have in common, and take for granted. The seminar was not about—and this collection of essays is not about—the meanings *of* the Bible, but about the Bible *and* meanings, about how modern and contemporary social identities and meanings and orientations are constructed, rationalized, and patterned in complex interactions with the Bible, and with what consequences.

The seminar afforded students the opportunity to define their projects as only the beginning of independent explorations of modern if not always contemporary complex situations in the United States in which the Bible plays some relevant and poignant, even disturbing roles. These beginnings of the students' explorations in *modern and contemporary society and culture*—as opposed to (in almost mantra-like reference) *"the (ancient) text"*—represented a radical departure from the, surprisingly, still rather conservative Protestant theological curriculum, in spite of the fact that the seminar was given the traditionally abbreviated designation for a *biblical field*, specifically a New Testament studies course offering.

This radical departure from the theological (and religious studies) curricular and scholarly guild norm reflects both problem and opportunity facing the contemporary academic study of the Bible. On the one hand, it points to the still mostly antiquarian orientation of the field—whether of the theological or historicist bent of the theological seminary/divinity school or the arts and sciences context. The shared assumption of this orientation is that the text and its pasts are where teaching and scholarship in the field should be focused; they are in fact thought of as the foundation of thinking and behavior. The problems inherent in this orientation are many; but it is enough to indicate here that the antiquarian orientation has become so entrenched, so much the baseline and touchstone, even across radical conservative and liberal divides, so adept at masking itself and practicing academic-religious obfuscation, that its presuppositions and agenda are hidden even from its fastidious practitioners.

Most problematic is that the entrenched naturalization of the orientation results in such keen sensitivity about the tightly patterned control (methods and approaches) of the enterprise—in service of and to protect God and church and academy it is claimed—that the range of questions (never mind *new* questions!) that can be addressed is sadly kept rather narrow. The result is a type of academic socialization the general and intended hallmarks of which are intellectual narrowness and rigidity ("Begin with the text . . . ") and timidity ("But those questions and issues are not in the text . . . "). That this situation also has severely restricted and continues to restrict who is allowed to play the game in the first place should be clear to all; given the functions of the Bible in Western culture in general and in American culture in particular, it certainly is one of the most dramatic and ironic examples of religious-cultural-academic politics.

On the other hand, the departure from the norm suggests possibilities for the academic study of the Bible that heretofore have not been aggressively pursued or encouraged to any significant degree, certainly not in the contexts in which the training of those who will assume positions of authority in terms of the interpretation of the Bible—either as professors/scholars of Bible or ordained clergy. Imagine what it might mean for those training for clerical leadership to be challenged to think deeply, systematically, and critically first about the different ways in which the Bible has already shaped and is continuing to shape their culture, including those local communities from which they have come and/or to which they are expected to return in positions of authority and leadership.

What if theology students were required to begin their study of the Bible as the study of the history of the Bible's interactions with their own communities and their sociocultural, psychocultural, politicoideological effects, including effects upon the interpreters? And what if such study were seen as springboard or impetus for the engagement of the ancient text as part of the agenda of rethinking and reconnecting society, culture, and religion? What if the theological studies curriculum were oriented not around the study of the canonical text, but around the study of the intellectual implications and socioreligious ramifications of the interactions of Bible and society and culture? The possibilities for reorientations, reconfigurations, and reconceptualizations abound.

I had asked my students to think about American culture (or parts of it) as a matrix within which their engagement of the Bible takes place, a filter through which their encounters with the Bible is necessarily mediated. I also sharpened the issue by asking students to ask whether, in what ways, and to what extent, the American myth had mediated the Bible for them and their communities. Selections of primary documents and provocative secondary interpretive works facilitated conversation and thinking among us. It was striking to discover the sheer breadth and depth, the imbeddedness, of the Bible *in* American culture, the interwovenness of the Bible *and* American culture. In so many different respects and with so many different consequences, American culture, on account of its texturalization, it can be said, is a biblical formation. From the naming of children, towns, and streets as a reflection of the most superficial of registrations, to the debates on the floors of Congress as an example of the ways in which the Bible is understood as an accessible ideological playing field used in order to legitimize different sociopolitical positions, to the widely shared and emotionally felt belief in "America" itself as God's "New Israel," "the shining City on a Hill," belated, primitive, exceptional, called to represent God in the new world order— all theses forms of engagement suggest that the Bible is fully implicated in the construction of the myth of American exceptionalism and divine mission. The pervasiveness of the myth in the culture, its perduring quality, its mixed and controversial, but always powerful, effects, inspired the seminar that inspired the collection of essays that follow.

Of course, it is not that there is no opposition to the American myth. Students found much evidence that there have always been those few who understood what the myth represented and opposed it; and it is also clear that there have been and remain those who by virtue of who they are and want to be, who they are represented to be by others, can never fully reflect or fully participate in the myth. Yet it can hardly be denied that the myth has been and remains powerful to the point that it must be conceded that it has set the terms for playing on the field of public debate about issues of the day, indeed, for successfully negotiating society and culture. From nineteenth-century views about slavery to contemporary bombings over the morality of late-term abortions and the rhetorics of political campaigns, the myth is very much a factor in American life.

This understanding and use of the Bible goes far beyond any debates, legal or otherwise, about the separation of church and state. What we confront in this matter is something deeper, more subtle, more complicit and interwoven in the very fabric of the culture. Referred to by Martin Marty to as "scripturality," it is the iconic use of the Bible that dramatically captures the ethos and orientation of the American republic and creates and essentially constitutes its public religion.[1] It is this republic and its dominant public religion that presses the Bible into the service that is the construction and maintenance of the American myth of exceptionalism and special call. The myth "works" because it represents a collection of ideas that are, according to Marty, "so deep that we do not even know we hold them. They are not the ideas that we 'have' but the ideas we 'are.' "[2] To use another metaphor to dramatic effect, they are ideas that function as a "carapace," "the protective covering . . . cocoon" for America's self-images and self-definitions.[3]

The recognition of the Bible as one of most powerful symbols and forces in the construction and deconstruction of the American myth and, in turn, of the American republic, society and culture, is only the first step in setting up a different agenda for the study of the Bible. The pluralism and differentiation of American society and culture—the pervasive infection and power of the myth notwithstanding—surely needs to be registered and taken seriously in terms of assumptions made and methods and approaches employed in the study of the Bible in America. The myth, after all, may be interpreted differently in different times and situations within the one (admittedly complex, differentiated) culture. And it may be interpreted differently in different subcultural sites of interpretation. Gender-specific and status-specific interpretations may also obtain within subcultural sites of interpretation. Without denying the reality of such differences, the American myth can be established as an explanatory frame of reference. Without it too much becomes inexplicable or too simplistic.

Insofar as the Bible is recognized as rather important in helping to accord legitimacy to the public religion in the United States, and insofar as the Bible continues to this day to be engaged by elites and nonelites alike through the prism of the American myth, the very meaning and agenda of and approaches to biblical interpretation for our times must change dramatically. Interpretation must

---

[1] See Martin E. Marty, *Religion and Republic: The American Circumstance* (Boston: Beacon Press, 1987) 142-43.

[2] Ibid., 141.

[3] Ibid., 146.

now be refocused—away from the text, onto society and culture. *We must no longer begin with the text, but with the people and their interactions with the text.* And we must no longer seek to make the claim that the end point, the baseline consideration, is the text. Such a claim is a ruse: it has more often than not been the dominant culture's interpretation of itself masked or certainly projected as (culture-sanctioned) *interpretation* of "sacred" text that has been the agenda. It is only when the culture is so taken for granted as reflection or reification of truth and reality and power that the text is foregrounded. The foregrounding of the text in terms of the attention to the details of the text (exegesis) then reflects the culture's shared views on the major issues—for example, on the matter of how reality is to be viewed, how truth is revealed and discerned—with only the fine points to be debated. Then a type of naturalization between text and society is established. Exegetes, intellectually and academically socialized in either state-supported institutions for state employment (the situation in Europe) or private elite institutions for private elite appointments (the situation in the United States), unless they are radically dis- or reoriented, can all too easily fall into the role of official shaman, holding the exegetical finger in the dike.

The essayists included in this volume have begun with society and culture—each with curiosity or particular theses to advance about a wide range of issues. These issues include a poignant historical controversy regarding the academic-critical approach to the Bible; the role of the Bible in fairly recent, rather dramatic, even violent, events involving fringe religious groups; the uses of the Bible in the self-definitions and orientations of contemporary racial-ethnic "minority" communities or peoples within the culture; the use of the Bible in the political construction of the myth of unity. All essayists have sought to understand and explain how the Bible as a whole functioned or functions in particular social-cultural situations. The focus upon any particular part of the Bible is the result of the registration of such focus on the part of those individuals or communities being studied. In this respect, the essays attempt to model the study of the Bible as the study of culture—the study of the construction and maintenance and complexification of society and culture and the functions of the Bible as a part of such dynamics. This collection is not the comprehensive, exhaustive treatment of any particular topic or even the original, definitive argument about or twist on any problem. It is instead an attempt to model a different point of departure for the study of the Bible in our times. It is the showcasing of a rather different orientation among students in a biblical studies course that commends, indeed, makes compelling, this collection of essays. It should, perhaps, be left to readers and reviewers over a period of time to determine the relationship between the students' openness to experimentation which must be properly understood as a radical point of departure—beginning not with "the text," but with society and culture—and their incomplete socialization into traditional academic biblical studies.

Should the project behind the collection of essays be considered *un*biblical studies, *anti*biblical studies? Who wants or needs biblical studies to be differently oriented? Who wants or needs the study of the Bible to be construed along the several lines suggested by the essays? What may be most provocative about this collection— not any one essay in isolation—is what a group of bright and energetic students in the context of a biblical studies course at a theological seminary may be communicating about what for them are the sorts of questions, issues, problems, methods, and approaches to which biblical studies should be open. In sum, the collection may be most important in what it reflects and signals about the interests and orientations of a small but in many ways highly representative group of theological and religious studies students for whom biblical studies means little unless it involves (among other things) culture studies, including the study of the worlds whence they come, within which they develop, over against which they struggle. For these student-essayists the Bible is a late-modern, not an ancient document.

There are many lessons here for theological and religious studies in broad scope, certainly for biblical studies. But some lessons it seems can be taught only by certain persons. In light of the pace of change in graduate programs in Bible in North America, I suggest that what is most compelling about this volume is that it represents the lessons that most probably could be conveyed only by the *types*—students of diverse backgrounds who by the historical demographic measure of any major graduate program in Bible in North America would be considered "new" to the field of biblical studies—who have contributed to it.

It was left to each student to choose the focus for these essays. Again, no claim for comprehensiveness or even originality of treatment of focus is being made. The essays do not intend to interpret the Bible or any of its parts per se. They aim not to interpret the meaning(s) *of* the Bible, but the Bible *and* meaning(s). What is being claimed is that the essays as a collection beg serious reconsideration of the dominant historical and literary-critical paradigm for the academic study of the Bible. Each essay also calls for a different orientation to the Bible and begs serious reconsideration of different parts of the Bible.

Andrea Smith's essay, "The American Way and the Good Red Road: American Indians, the Christian Right, and the (De)Construction of the American Religion," is an examination of the role of the Bible in the construction and legitimation of the contemporary dominant American religion, and the relationships that obtain between the representatives of the dominant circle, different peoples and groups outside the dominant circle, and the Bible. The latter as site of contestation/deconstruction of the dominant circle and the interpretation/construction of alternate selves and cultures is made explicit, and thereby begs sharper thinking about interpretation and positionality.

Harold Rhee's essay, " 'It's a Small World . . . ': Abraham Lincoln, the New American Myth and the Biblical Rhetoric of Unity," reexamines a rather long-standing American tradition of drawing upon biblical rhetoric in order to effect and maintain a degree of social cohesion. In the manner in which it raises questions about Lincoln's construction and artful employment of such a hermeneutic as well as some of its lingering effects, Rhee's essay also raises haunting issues and questions about the interpretation of a number of favorite American biblical references.

Doug Hill's essay entitled "Charles Augustus Briggs, Modernism, and the Rise of Biblical Scholarship in Nineteenth-Century America," a cultural-critical study of pioneer American historical critic Charles Briggs, begs rethinking about the entire enterprise that is the historical-critical approach to the study of the Bible.

Examination of Briggs's personal motivations and the social-ecclesi-astical-technological-cultural matrices and dynamics within which his challenge to premodern interpretation of the Bible took place throws the beginnings and development of the critical approach to the study of the Bible, in the United States in particular, in arresting and ironic relief.

Kimberleigh Jordan's essay, "The Body as Reader: African-Americans, Freedom, and the American Myth," challenges the popular understanding that the dominant American myth is about freedom and liberty, that freedom and liberty have been realized in American society, and that the myth and the social reality can be viewed as simply inspired by the Bible. Through focus upon the historical and enduring plight of African-Americans, especially African-American women, the essay also challenges approaches to the study of the Bible and of society and culture that would leave the myth unbroken and unchallenged. With the notion of the body as reader and with focus upon the Old Testament story of Hagar, the essay provokes thinking about means other than through the dominant American myth to explore freedom and liberty in American society.

David Saul's essay, "Children of the American Myth: David Koresh, the Branch Davidians, and the American Bible," dramatically makes the case for the Branch Davidians as deadly accurate modern-day tradents of the predominant American myth and the role of the Bible in its construction and legitimation. Saul argues that a critical reconsideration of some favorite American biblical texts through the prism of the American myth and of the American myth through reconsideration of some biblical texts, is needed for the sake of obtaining a more critical grasp of self-construction.

Rosamond Rodman's contribution, "Heaven's Gate: Religious Outworldliness American Style," is also a study of a fairly recent subcultural group and a challenge to reconsider what is the long-standing characteristic American identification, translation, and social-cultural reification of the dominant orientations of the Bible, with their frightening and breathtaking ramifications and heady hermeneutical and cultural-critical implications. According to Rodman, some biblical books and passages that have become and remain obvious American favorites now demand from the perspectives of specifically *American* self-understandings a different sort of critical exegesis—of the culture as text and of the text encultured.

Charles Mabee's essay is in one respect a response to the conversation that the collection of student essays represents. But his essay is less a critique of any one argument advanced by an essayist; it is instead an extension of the arguments, an example of the addressing of some of the issues in ways that the essays suggest.

In another respect, of course, Mabee's essay is a response to the collection of essays that is a type of response to his own well-regarded work in the area of American biblical hermeneutics. Although the entry point for my own thinking about American biblical hermeneutics has been through African-American cultural expressivities and in terms of culture broadly understood, it has been clear to me for several years that my work could benefit from that of Mabee's. This collection and the seminar behind it drew upon and entered into conversation with Mabee's work in a serious way.

But the politics of the academy and of ecclesiastical discursiveness needs to be acknowledged and problematized here if only for the sake of indicating in another way what might be the import of this collection. Although Mabee's academic pedigree is superb, and although his scholarship is without question learned and respected, creative and provocative, it needs to be said that the fact that his professorial appointment is *not* at an institution with a graduate program in Old Testament/Hebrew Bible is telling—and chilling. What are the politics and hermeneutics of this situation? I suggest that what is at issue is more than the usual academic market forces: the very issues that Mabee has made the general focus of his scholarship—American biblical hermeneutics—and the theme of this collection—the Bible and construction of social meanings— are pertinent here. Graduate programs in Bible, headquartered primarily in theological seminaries and divinity schools, are still at century's end very conservative in their response to outside impulses and fairly resistant to the clamor for change. Whether falling back upon what is repetitively and thus nauseatingly claimed to be the "church's" interests or what is timidly asserted to be the academy's demands, change in the these programs has been resisted. Surely not unrelated to this matter is the fact that these programs—*Nota bene*: we are talking here about the Bible in America!—can hardly function as commercials for diversity in higher education. Mabee's construal of the study of the Bible as the study of American cultural hermeneutics is a significant challenge to graduate programs in "Bible" in North America.

How should my institutional placement and professional survival be explained? Perhaps it is best to allow others to hold forth more fully about the matter. As far as I can determine I am, if not the first biblical scholar, then certainly among the first of biblical scholars with a professorial appointment in a "mainline" institution with a graduate program in Bible to offer courses on the Bible and American culture. The distinctions and qualifications are by no means unimportant! Although I have long been associated with interests related to Bible and culture, it is very clear to me that such interests have not heretofore been encouraged or supported by peers or deemed relevant or important. The questions whether such interests and courses were, and whether I was any longer, "in the field" have been heard often enough to make the point about what is at stake.

So the significance of the collection that follows cannot be overstressed. The student-essayists of different backgrounds located at the mouth of Harlem at the turn of the century indicate below that they want to think of the Bible in connection with who and what they are, namely, in connection with culture—its construction, deconstruction, and reconstruction. In this respect, they also reflect the strong impulse toward making the radical shift in focus in the study of religion and theology from interpretation of texts to the interpretation of world, of culture (with sensitivity to the effects of the textualization of culture). What such a shift in focus opens up for investigation and questioning in the area of culture studies and religion in the context of theological and religious studies programs we can only now begin to imagine. But what readers will see below is that the students shall—perhaps only they can—lead us. Therein may lie the most important contribution of this collection.

The American Way and the Good Red Road: American Indians, the Christian Right, and the (De)Construction of American Religion

Andrea Smith

Introduction
The American Religion

In *The American Religion*, Harold Bloom notes that "The God of the American Religion is not a creator-God, because the American never *was* created, and so the American has at least part of the God within herself."[1] In other words, the American religion—and, by extension, America—understands itself as a phenomenon that is at once eternal and without history; it is unaware of its own social constructedness. "American Religion, which is nothing if not a *knowing*, does not know itself."[2] Ironically, while *The American Religion* presents itself as descriptive discourse on the "essence of religion," it is a performative discourse as well: as he (de)scribes "American Religion" as an essentialized, noncreated phenomenon, Bloom unconsciously reinscribes the notion by failing to ask *who* created the American Religion. In Bloom's account, a host of other faiths all "to some degree . . . share in the American Religion, how-

---

[1] Harold Bloom, *The American Religion. The Emergence of the Post-Christian Nation* (New York: Simon & Schuster, 1992) 114.
[2] Ibid., 263.

ever unknowingly or unwillingly,"[3] but none seems to have had a hand in fashioning it. Do these groups simply experience the "American Religion" passively, or is it something they *do*? Is the American Religion the same now as it was before, say, the Mormons, or are the Mormons partly responsible for its current shape?

Marshall Blonsky's *American Mythologies* focuses on "American mythologies" rather than on American religion, but it covertly participates in a similar essentializing discourse: "For the moment we [Americans] produce the myths . . . and Europeans, Russians, and Japanese are eager to interpret, reject, or assimilate them."[4] Although Blonsky's myths have a history, their production seems to take place in a homogenous, and almost exclusively white America that *already* expresses, as it were, the American essence. Blonsky's Europeans, Russians, and Japanese are simply outsiders and myth consumers: while they do have the power to "interpret, reject, or assimilate" American myths, they never manage to penetrate the boundaries of American culture; they, therefore, have no hand in reshaping these myths according to their interpreting, rejecting, and assimilating labors. Moreover, the myths themselves never seem to loop back into the American consciousness with any (re)creative force.

In this essay, I shall examine some of the dynamics of constructing and deconstructing both American and Christian identity by focusing upon two communities—the Christian Right and American Indians—and how their uses of the Bible help to define their relationship to "America." First, I fathom how the doctrine of biblical inerrancy figures both implicitly and explicitly in Christian Right discourse, and more specifically, how in certain sectors of the Christian Right, adherence to biblical inerrancy symbolizes "true Americanism," which in turn symbolizes adherence to a particular set of conservative political beliefs. For other sectors of the Christian Right, however, adherence to biblical inerrancy troubles any easy connection between the Bible, America, and conservative politics.

---

[3]Ibid., 28.
[4]Marshall Blonsky, *American Mythologies* (New York: Oxford University Press, 1992) 13.

Next, using American Indians as a case example, I shall note how biblical inerrancy serves to marginalize many communities from inclusion in evangelical Christian discourse. I shall next look at various readings of resistance to both the Bible and America within Indian communities. Ironically, while Indian evangelicals may adhere to doctrinal beliefs similar to those of the white Christian Right, their seemingly "assimilationist" readings of the Bible often serve the goals of Indian rather than U.S. nationalism. Indian nationalists, by contrast, attempt to deconstruct both the Bible and America, but their seemingly oppositional readings often unconsciously legitimize or "legitimate" Christian America.

The Christian Right and American Indian readings of both the Bible and America demonstrate the problems inherent in categorizing readings as either constructive or deconstructive. These readings suggest an additional mode of analysis—how do constructive readings unintentionally subvert that which they claim to support, and how do deconstructive readings implicitly uphold that which they critique? These readings also problematize some analyses of American myth making proposed by both Blonsky and Bloom. "America" is not a transhistorical phenomenon which is simply rejected, supported, or imposed upon communities. Rather, communities actively take part in the process of creating "America"— even when they reject it.

I will conclude with an alternative Native reading of the Bible and Christian America that recognizes this complex interplay of constructive and deconstructive readings. This approach does not rely on an essentializing discourse about either American Indians or Christian America. This reading does not seek inclusion within Christian American discourse. Nor does it attempt to replace it with another competing discourse. Rather, it seeks to decenter Christian American myths from their hegemonic position by recontextualizing them within American Indian myths of origin.

Part 1
The Christian Right, the Bible, and America

The Civil Gospel

David Barton heads WallBuilders, an organization "dedicated to rebuilding God's principles in public affairs." WallBuilders promotes what James Guth describes as a "civil gospel," which is a Christian Right rationale for political involvement. "This theology argues that the US was founded as a Christian nation but has fallen from that status, and Christian citizens must take action to protect their own rights and restore the American constitutional system and buttress morality."[5] In analyzing a few essays from *WallBuilder Report* as an example of a civil gospel, it is possible to discern how the doctrine of biblical inerrancy, a hallmark of evangelical Christianity,[6] functions as a signifier of not only what is "truly" Christian, but also what is "truly" American. True Christianity and true Americanism, in turn, signify an adherence to certain uncontestable conservative political positions.

---

[5]James Guth, "The Bully Pulpit," in *Religion and the Culture Wars: Dispatches from the Front*, ed. John Green et al. (Lanham MD: Rowman and Littlefield, 1996) 160.

[6]There are many definitions in circulation of both evangelical Christianity and the Christian Right. I define the Christian Right as evangelical Christians who tend toward conservative politics (although they may disagree about the extent to which they think they should engage in politics). By "evangelical," I mean primarily Protestants who generally subscribe to the five "fundamentals" of faith that have served as rallying points for evangelicalism: biblical inerrancy; the deity of Christ; substitutionary atonement; bodily resurrection; and the Second Coming of Christ. This definition is inclusive of Pentecostals and those groups that do not trace their roots to the fundamentalist/modernist debates of the 1920s. I am not including the more explicitly racist Christian movements, such as Christian identity groups. See Ronald Nash, *Evangelicals in America* (Nashville: Abingdon, 1987); William Trollinger, "How Should Evangelicals Understand Fundamentalism?" *United Evangelical Action* 44 (September–October 1985): 7-9; Edward Dobson, "Standing Together on Absolutes," *United Evangelical Action* 44 (September–October 1985): 4-10; Harold J. Ockenga, "From Fundamentalism through New Evangelicalism to Evangelicalism" *Evangelical Roots* (Nashville: Thomas Nelson, 1968); and Donald Dayton, *The Variety of American Evangelicalism* (Knoxville: University of Tennessee Press, 1991).

Those who advocate inerrancy take the Bible in its plain and obvious sense.... All that is meant by saying one takes the Bible literally is that one believes what it purports to say.[7]

As Kathleen Boone notes in *The Bible Tells Them So*, evangelicalism claims itself as a discourse unimpeded by social realities. That is, evangelicals claim to be speaking only biblical truth, repeating the inerrant word of God. The biblical text exists outside the bounds of other social discourses. While evangelicals claim this, there is not a single evangelical interpretation of any biblical text. Thus, the question is, what are the parameters that bound acceptable evangelical discourse, and who defines these parameters?

No matter how much one may claim to take the Bible as one's authority, one is judged by one's fidelity to the fundamentalist interpretative model. That allegiance established, it seems that one may apply biblical texts to life circumstances and situations with considerable freedom.[8]

Evangelical biblical discourse claims to be unchanging and suprahistorical. So according to Barton: "The Bible has been transcendent across generations and cultures, and its guidance has remained timeless."[9] Furthermore, the true meaning of the Bible is self-evident to any reader of it.

Barton describes the U.S. Constitution in a similar fashion, taking issue with legal scholars who wish to adapt constitutional principles to contemporary society, rather than to abide by the original intent of the Founding Fathers. For instance, some legal scholars might identify general constitutional principles, such as justice or fairness, as guiding principles to decide issues that are not covered in the Constitution, such as gay rights. According to Barton, this approach is incorrect. If the Founding Fathers did not mention gay rights in the Constitution in the 1700s, then gays

---

[7]Harold Lindsell, *Battle of the Bible* (Grand Rapids MI: Zondervan, 1976) 37.

[8]Kathleen C. Boone, *The Bible Tells Them So: The Discourse of Protestant Fundamentalism* (Albany: SUNY P:ress, 1989) 89. Note that Boone subsumes the evangelical into the fundamentalist world.

[9]David Barton, "The Shifting Paradigm: Where Will It End?" *WallBuilder Report* (Fall 1994): 5.

should not be protected by the Constitution today. It is not important that the social/cultural context of the authors of both the Bible and the Constitution are completely different from today or that issues of concern to us today were not even a consideration to these authors during their time; we must guide our lives and our country based on what these writers prescribed. Somehow, these authors were able to transcend their sociopolitical context and write documents that are correct, changing contexts notwithstanding.

The Constitution seems to assume almost an equal status to the Bible within the discourse of the civil gospel. Its authors are deemed godly men whose personal lives are beyond reproach. To prove this point, WallBuilders has published an entire book dedicated to establishing the virtuousness and the morality of the Founding Fathers.[10] The implicit goal of this book is to show that the founding fathers were not limited by personal biases, self-interest, or prejudices, and consequently, neither is the Constitution. Insofar as the Founding Fathers wrote a constitution based on biblical principles, the author of the Constitution is in fact God. To stray from the Constitution is to stray from the Bible, and ultimately to stray from God. Barton quotes George Washington, arguing "that the propitious smiles of Heaven can never be expected on a nation that disregards the eternal rules of order and right which Heaven itself has ordained."[11]

Implicit in this argument about the proper interpretive approach to both the Bible and the Constitution is that the original intent of the authors is self-evident. As Boone explains this discourse, "If the Bible is the sole authority for fundamentalists, it must be accessible to every reader. If there is to be no institutional authority in interpretation, it follows that no such authority can be considered necessary."[12] The Constitution similarly requires no institution such as the Supreme Court to interpret it. In fact, many

---

[10]Barton. "The Race Card," *WallBuilder Report* (Fall 1995): 1-7.

[11]From WallBuilders promotional material (corrected to conform to the original). Barton admits he fabricates quotations—see discussion below—but this quotation is indeed from George Washington, namely, from his first inaugural address (to Congress), on 30 April 1789.

[12]Boone, *The Bible Tells Them So*, 17.

Christian Right organizations, including the WallBuilders, call for restricting the powers of the Supreme Court; they claim the Court fails to interpret the obvious meaning of the Constitution.[13] As Barton puts it, the way to contest those who wish to contextualize the meanings of both the Constitution and the Bible is to "simply [teach] others what is right."[14] Consequently, the conservative political positions that should result from the correct interpretation of both the Bible and the Constitution do not require justification because they are clearly evident within both documents.

Ironically, because these positions are supposedly so evident within the Bible and the Constitution, it is not necessary for Christian Right advocates even to reference these positions. For example, Barton describes abortion and condom distribution as biblical issues without any constitutional or biblical references.[15] Using a similar rhetorical strategy, the National Association of Evangelicals passed a resolution on the topic of partial-birth abortions this year, which originally stated that "The National Association of Evangelicals affirms the declarations of Scripture that all human life is a sacred gift from a Sovereign God and that partial-birth abortion is a great moral wrong."[16] Interestingly, during the deliberations over the resolution, one man challenged this language, arguing that he had "looked all through the Bible and I didn't find any mention about partial-birth abortions."[17] So, the language was changed to "The National Association of Evangelicals affirms the declarations of Scripture that all human life is a sacred gift from a Sovereign God. Therefore, partial-birth abortion is a great moral wrong."[18]

This episode reflected a moment of self-awareness among some evangelicals at the NAE that they were using the Bible to symbol-

---

[13]See, e.g., "Reader's Response," *Christian American* 8 (May/June 1997): 8.

[14]Barton, "Shifting Paradigm," 7.

[15]David Barton, "Inside the 1996 Elections," *WallBuilder Report* (Winter 1997): 1.

[16]"Resolution on Partial Birth Abortions," National Association of Evangelicals, 4 March 1997.

[17]National Association of Evangelicals Conference, Orlando Florida, 4 March 1997.

[18]"Resolution on Partial Birth Abortions."

ize a political posture that the Bible itself did not address. Of course, this awareness was limited by the fact that the final resolution did not contain any biblical reference that all human life is sacred. Nor was there any debate about whether a ban on partial-birth abortion necessarily results from the first presupposition. Thus, while there is no clear mandate in the U.S. Constitution or the Bible that specifically calls Christians to oppose abortion, support welfare repeal, or support immigration restrictions, the civil gospel's appeals to biblical and constitutional inerrancy seem to connote these positions; alternative positions are not truly Christian or American. The Bible is significant for what it represents, not for what it says. Fundamentalists hold what Martin Marty describes as "the iconic regard for the Bible as an object in the national shrine, whether read or not, whether observed or not: it is seen as being basic to national and religious communities' existence."[19]

While Barton appeals to the plain and correct meanings of both the Bible and the Constitution to guide society, his own arguments demonstrate that "plain and correct meanings" never transcend their interpretive context. While Barton complains about "revisionist" history that does not teach students what "really" happened, he has also admitted that most of the "historical" documents he uses to prove the Christian heritage of the Founding Fathers are entirely bogus.[20]

His discussion of slavery is another case in point. A "plain" reading of both the Bible and the Constitution would seem to suggest that their respective authors either explicitly or implicitly approved of slavery and the authors of the Constitution supported white supremacy. However, according to Barton, the plain meaning is not so obvious after all. He argues that the 3/5 compromise section of the Constitution is actually pro-Black! "[T]he truth is that it was the Founders who were responsible for planting and nurturing the first seeds for the recognition of black equality and

---

[19]Martin E. Marty, *Religion and Republic: The American Circumstance* (Boston: Beacon Press, 1987) 164.

[20]Rob Boston, "Consumer Alert! WallBuilders' Shoddy Workmanship," *Church and State* 49 (July/August 1996): 11-13.

for the eventual end of slavery."[21] This example illustrates the unacknowledged politics of biblical and constitutional inerrancy. While Barton decries "evolutionary" approaches to constitutional law, his interpretation of slavery in the Constitution depends upon an evolutionary approach to public policies regarding racism and slavery. That is, he is arguing that the constitutional and biblical position on slavery should not be the same today as it was in the 1700s—the position set forth by the Founding Fathers is not the one we should follow today. Yet, were other readers to adopt this contextualizing hermeneutic for other issues, such as abortion or gay rights, they would misunderstand the "true" meaning of the Constitution. This contradiction is similar for many conservative evangelical scholars, such as those represented by Christians for Biblical Manhood and Womanhood, who make arguments akin to Barton's about slavery in the Bible, but then condemn evangelical feminists who apply the same principles to patriarchy.[22] Thus, while proponents of the civil gospel would direct us to the "plain and correct" meaning of the Bible and the Constitution, clearly not all readers of these documents have equal authority to ascertain these "plain" meanings.

Within the discourse of the civil gospel as exemplified by the WallBuilders, the doctrine of biblical inerrancy serves to signify a Christian America. "Christian America," in turn, signifies a collection of conservative political positions on a variety of issues judged to be "biblically" and "constitutionally" based (the two almost equated within this discourse) and as such are considered to be beyond debate.

"Let Christian America Rest in Peace"

It is important to note that while the civil gospel seems to suggest an inevitable marriage between biblical inerrancy and conservative politics, this marriage in fact has been a recent historical development. Until the rise of such organizations as the Moral Majority, conservative evangelical/fundamentalists often tended to

---

[21]David Barton, "The Race Card," *WallBuilder Report* (Fall 1995): 7.
[22]See, e.g., John Piper and Wayne Grudem, *Recovering Biblical Manhood and Womanhood* (Wheaton IL: Crossway Books, 1991) 65-66.

refrain from electoral politics. George Marsden notes that the rise of fundamentalism during the early 1900s was partly a reaction against the Social Gospel's emphasis on social activism. While the social gospel attempted to reform the social structures of the day, fundamentalism held no hope that humans could change their inherently corrupt society. Fundamentalists believed the only hope was for "salvation" of an individual rather than on a collective basis. In their view, "No longer was the goal to build a 'perfect society,' at best it was to restrain evil until the Lord returned."[23] The more recent politicization of right-wing evangelical voters was engineered primarily by secular right activists, particularly Richard Viguerie and Paul Weyrich, who courted clergy persons such as Jerry Falwell to start the Moral Majority in order to mobilize the previously apolitical conservative evangelical vote.[24] As Michael Lienesch states: "At least at its inception, the New Christian Right, far from being a populist uprising, was an army organized from the top down by those New Right strategists who set much of the early agenda for their politically less sophisticated recruits."[25]

As Rob McKinniss's essay "Let 'Christian America' Rest in Peace" suggests, not all evangelicals favor a marriage between conservative politics and conservative theology.[26] McKinniss does not

---

[23]George M. Marsden, *Fundamentalism and American Culture: The Shaping of Twentieth Century Evangelicalism, 1870–1925* (London, New York: Oxford University Press, 1980) 31.

[24]See Sara Diamond, *Spiritual* Warfare (Boston: South End Press, 1989) 60; William C. Martin, *With God on Our Side: The Rise of Religious Right in America* (New York: Broadway Books, 1996); Ellen Rosenberg, *The Southern Baptists: A Subculture in Transition* (Knoxville: University of Tennessee Press, 1984); Duane Murray Oldfield, *The Right and the Righteous. The Christian Right Confronts the Republican Party* (Lanham MD: Rowman & Littlefield, 1996) 100; and James Guth, "The Politics of the Christian Right," in *Religion and the Culture Wars*, 15.

[25]Michael Lienesch, *Redeeming America. Piety and Politics in the New Christian Right* (Chapel Hill: University of North Carolina Press, 1993) 8.

[26]Robert McKinniss, "Let 'Christian America' Rest in Peace," *Christianity Today* 32 (15 February 1988): 10. Helmut Thielicke, "The Great Temptation," repr. in *Christianity Today* 29 (12 July 1985): 26-31; John Woodbridge, "Why Words Matter," *Christianity Today* 39 (19 June 1995): 31. Bob Briner laments that "Sadly, Christians are much more willing to finance a right-wing political effort than any spiritual one." Bob Briner, *Deadly Detours. Seven Noble Causes That Keep Christians from Changing the World* (Grand Rapids MI: Zondervan, 1996) 33.

advocate abandoning all social/political activism, but he does argue that Christians should ultimately invest themselves in the eschatological kingdom of God. America, according to McKinniss, is not Christian but is a "pagan land."[27] Biblical principles are not realized in the U.S. Constitution or in "America," but stand in judgment of them. Unlike Barton, McKinniss argues that the Founding Fathers were not Christian and had no intent of creating a Christian nation.

At a Christianity Today Institute on Church and the State, evangelical theologians agreed that "they are opposed to a Christian government that mandates 'Christian' laws simply because they are Christian" they also agreed that the "wall of separation between the church and state is good." There were also many disagreements as to whether ministers should be involved in politics. "The Christian as Citizen," *Christianity Today* 29 (19 April 1985): 28. When Tim LaHaye made a comment that conservative Christians had been "legislated out of the possibility of a spiritual revival" ("Leaders of the Christian Right Announce Their Next Step," *Christianity Today* 29 [13 December 1985]: 65), he received a deluge of angry letters chastising him for putting an inordinate investment in the legislative process rather than trusting in God. "Letters," *Christianity Today* 30 (7 February 1986): 10-11. Even conservative evangelist Luis Palau says North Americans should not "ask how to spread capitalism or democracy, but how to spread the gospel." He maintains that those in the Third World are "in the best position to decide how the gospel is contextualized." It is interesting that while he rejects Christian efforts at progressive social change, he also seems to reject the Westernization process of the Christian Right. Luis Palau, "Evangelism: The Best Form of Social Action," *Christianity Today* 33 (17 February 1990): 51-52. Carl F. H. Henry states: "Evangelicals must break out of their cultural ghettos to demand social change, affirm that a better social order is possible in our own time. . . . Failure to elaborate such an alternative will enable the champions of socialism, however self-defeating that option actually is, to win the war of "theological" ideas by default." Carl. F. H. Henry, "Insights on Liberation Theology," *United Evangelical Action* 45 (March–April 1986): 4-6. However, Henry also states: "Christians engage vulnerably in political and cultural activity if they merely presuppose the legitimacy of some prevalent view of the nature and mission of the church and concentrate their energies on social involvement. The cost of such engagement can be appalling, because the world easily penetrates and neutralizes a constituency unsure of its own nature and mission." Henry, in Richard Mouw, "Preaching Christ or Packaging Jesus?" *Christianity Today* 35 (11 February 1991): 38. Daniel J. Evearitt states: "those who expect a capitalist utopia will be disappointed. . . . we Christians should be cautioned against attaching our Christian faith too closely to any person, any political party, or any agenda. We are to be the Church. Our mission is always beyond specific political parties or ideological movements or personalities." *Rush Limbaugh and the Bible* (Camp Hill PA: Horizon House, 1993) 190.

[27]McKinniss, "Let 'Christian America' Rest in Peace," 10.

Ironically, this separation is to the benefit of Christianity. When Christianity weds itself to a nationalistic agenda, argues McKinniss, the specificity of the Christian message becomes diluted: "Impassioned cries for school prayer take little notice that the model prayers suggested do considerable damage to any Christian concept of the Deity and to the practice of prayer."[28] According to McKinniss, the priority of Christians should not be to advance "Christian" political positions, but to evangelize. The church operates not through civil government but through conversion of individual hearts to Christ. "Part of the genius of the church is its capacity to operate apart from set geographical boundaries, cultural biases, or national governments."[29] It is important to note that McKinniss maintains his patriotism; however, his adherence to biblical principles relativizes this patriotism. His final allegiance can never be to the "kingdom of America," but only to the kingdom of God, which stands in judgement of all other kingdoms. While America may fulfill *some* of the biblical requirements for a Christian Nation, the only true Christian nation is not of this world. America is only "a partly Christian nation."[30]

This critique is not unique among those in Christian Right circles. J. Alfred Smith, Sr. criticizes the trend toward "baptizing the United States as being God's chosen nation as a distortion of kingdom ethics. It presents . . . a sub-Christian display of the affluence and arrogance of American power."[31] James Skillen notes: "Pro-American conservatives . . . have not built a solid, political program around a political perspective that is grounded in biblical revelation. . . . [They] have offered neither a convincing rationale for the *Christian* character of America nor a principled Christian view of government and citizenship in a differentiated society."[32] Tim Stafford tells evangelical Christians to learn a lesson from Hitler and look out for right-wing demagogues who can play con-

---

[28]Ibid., 10.

[29]Ibid.

[30]Ibid.

[31]In "Listening to America's Ethnic Churches," *Christianity Today* 33 (3 March 1989): 33.

[32]James W. Skillen, *The Scattered Voice: Christians at Odds in the Public Square* (Grand Rapids MI: Zondervan, 1990) 53.

servative Christians "like a fiddle."[33] Billy Graham has also criticized Jerry Falwell, stating that it "it would disturb me if there was a wedding between religious fundamentalists and the political right. The hard right has no interest in religion except to manipulate it."[34]

The entry of fundamentalist pastors in the political realm during the 1980s created much controversy among fundamentalists and evangelicals because it required some in these ranks to make coalitions with non-Christians and to make compromises in order to become effective players in electoral politics. Such alliances have prompted militant fundamentalist Bob Jones to denounce Jerry Falwell as "the most dangerous man in America today as far as biblical Christianity is concerned."[35] Since then, as conservative Christians have become more politically sophisticated, the mantle of Christian Right leadership has been passed from ministers such as Jerry Falwell and Ed McAteer to political activists such as Ralph Reed and the members of the Christian Coalition. These new leaders and organizations care even less about doctrinal correctness than did their predecessors and more about building effective coalitions. Coalitions by nature cannot be doctrinally pure and will rankle constituents for whom such purity as represented by notions of biblical inerrancy is paramount. Many figures on the Christian Right have made alliances with groups such the Moonies and Mormons that are generally thought of as heretical by evangelicals, and these alliances have caused much dissension in Christian Right ranks.[36] The Christian Coalition, for example, is often described by evangelicals as a "wholly owned subsidiary of

---

[33]Tim Stafford, "Angel of Light," *Christianity Today* 33 (8 September 1989): 19.

[34]Billy Graham, "Billy Graham Speaks Out On Jerry Falwell," *CALC Report* 12 (December 1986): 27.

[35]Quoted in Walter H. Capps, *The New Religious Right: Piety, Patriotism, and Politics* (Columbia: University of South Carolina Press, 1994; 1990) 99.

[36]Tim LaHaye and other Christian Right leaders have received much scrutiny and criticism for working with the Unification Church, which at one point bankrolled a Christian Right organization, Christian Voice. Beth Spring, "Magazine Says Tim LaHaye Received Help from Unification Church," *Christianity Today* 30 (17 January 1986): 40-41; Kim Lawton, "Unification Church Ties Haunt New Coalition," *Christianity Today* 32 (5 February 1988): 46-47.

the Republican Party."[37] Clark Cochran of Texas Tech complained that the agenda is "just a secular political agenda with a Christian stamp."[38] Former Moral Majoritarian Ed Dobson agrees: "I think they [the Christian Coalition] ought to drop the religious attachment to their organization and just admit they're a conservative political group, but since [the Christian Coalition was] birthed in the environment of religious commitment, it's hard to drop that."[39]

Thus, while promoters of the civil gospel espouse a marriage between the Bible and the U.S. Constitution, the evocation of the "literal" word of God at the same time threatens the marriage between the Christian Right and political conservativism. Adherence to the "literal" word of God suggests a relativizing of U.S. institutions. The attempt to mobilize Christians in order to restore the Christian nature of America inevitably contributes to the necessity of working with people of other faiths, which in turn leads to a relativizing or marginalizing of the Bible, which is supposed to have inspired this political activism in the first place. Duane Oldfield describes this fault line of Christian Right organizing:

> The Christian Right confronts a difficult dilemma: to gain public acceptability, build alliances, and effectively promote its political agenda, it needs to downplay divisive religious doctrine and express its case in more secular terms, in terms likely to find favor in the public realm of politics. Yet such a strategy is likely to undermine the religious enthusiasm and organization upon which the movement and its leaders have built their fortunes.[40]

Consequently, the more a Christian organization seems willing to compromise on "biblical" principles in order to increase its political effectiveness, the more criticism it meets. For instance, Southern Baptist clergy have given the Christian Coalition a thirty-four percent approval rate (as compared to eighty-four percent for Focus on the Family—a Christian Right organization that is less compro-

---

[37]Ralph Reed, *After the Revolution: How the Christian Coalition Is Impacting America* (Dallas: Word Books, 1996) 245.

[38]Joe Loconte, "Will the Religious Right Gain Momentum in 1994?" *Christianity Today* 38 (7 February 1994): 51, 53.

[39]Quoted in Martin, *With God on Our Side*, 365.

[40]Oldfield, *The Right and the Righteous*, 72.

mising on such issues as abortion, but which also lacks the influence of the Christian Coalition in electoral politics).[41] As Ed McAteer, president of the Religious Roundtable, states, there is a "difference between coalition building and accommodating atheists."[42]

Biblical inerrancy, then, has an ambivalent effect upon Christian Right discourse. Among those who promote a civil gospel inerrancy signifies a certain set of conservative political positions, even though these positions cannot actually be defended by anything in the Bible itself. At the same time, many evangelicals find that biblical inerrancy requires them to distance themselves from political concerns because any political program would require some dilution of "biblical principles" to gain popular and institutional support. In sum, in evangelical discourse biblical inerrancy can serve both to construct and to deconstruct Christian America.

Part 2
Native Responses
to the Christian Right's Christian America

It is important to consider who qualifies as a Christian American among the various proponents of a civil gospel—certainly not everyone who calls himself/herself either "Christian" or "American," and certainly not everyone who lives in the geographic space of America. I want now to look at one community that generally finds itself at the margins of this discourse, American Indians, and note how its relationship to the Bible and the Constitution serves to destabilize Christian Right discourses on inerrancy and Americanism. I will then look at two types of Native readings of Christian America and the Bible: evangelical/"assimilationist" and traditional/"oppositional" approaches.

There's no question that white evangelical Protestants, especially in the South, were not only on the sidelines but were on the

---

[41]John Green, "A Look at the Invisible Army," in *Religion and the Culture Wars*, 58-59.

[42]As quoted by Randy Frame, "Were Christians Courted for Their Votes or Beliefs?" *Christianity Today* 33 (17 February 1989): 38-39.

wrong side of the most central struggle for civil justice of the twentieth century, namely the struggle for civil rights . . . until the pro-family, religious conservative movement becomes a truly biracial or multiracial movement, it will not have moral resonance with the American people, because we were so wrong at that time. I want the Christian Coalition to be a truly rainbow coalition. I want it to be black, brown, yellow, white. I want it to bring Christians of all faith traditions, all denominations, and all races and colors together. I don't think that's going to happen overnight. It's going to take years, but we're committed to it.[43]

This statement by Ralph Reed reflects a growing concern among the Christian Right regarding the issue of race reconciliation. Now evangelical Christian organizations everywhere, including the Promise Keepers, the National Association of Evangelicals, the Pentecostal Fellowship of North America, the National Religious Broadcasters, the Christian Coalition, and the Southern Baptist Convention, are jumping onto the race reconciliation bandwagon.[44] The purpose of race reconciliation, as Tony Evans puts it,

---

[43]Quoted in Martin, *With God on Our Side*, 365-66.

[44]When Bill McCartney organized the first Promise Keepers (PK) rally in 1991, he was troubled by the fact that the attendees were all white: "The Spirit of God clearly said to my spirit, 'You can fill that stadium, but if men of other races aren't there, I won't be there, either." Since then, McCartney has made race reconciliation one of the top priorities of the Promise Keepers, and his efforts seem to be meeting with some success. While in general about 84% of the attendees at PK rallies are white, at the 1996 rally in New York City, one-third to one-half of the attendees were men of color. (Sheldon King, "We Must Come Together," *New Man* 4 [January/February 1997]: 24.) Typically, about one-third to one-half of speakers at PK rallies are men of color, and racial themes sound throughout most if not all speeches. PK's journal, *New Man*, also focuses on race reconciliation and prominently features articles by and about men of color—more so than left-leaning journals like the *Nation* and the *Progressive*.

More than a dozen books on race reconciliation were published in 1996 by evangelical publishers, and Bill Anderson, president of the Christian Booksellers Association, directly attributes the increased visibility of African-American authors in CBA stores to the Promise Keepers. (Steve Rabey, "Where Is the Christian Men's Movement Headed?" *Christianity Today* 40 [29 April 1996]: 60.) In 1995, the Southern Baptist Convention issued an apology for slavery and racism. Emmanuel McCall, an African-American in the Southern Baptist Home Mission Board, recently declared "the Southern Baptist Convention the most racially inclusive religious body in America." ("About-face on Race," *Christianity Today* [n.d. 1990]: 46.) The mostly white Pentecostal Fellowship of North America

is to "establish a church where everyone of any race or status who walks through the door is loved and respected as part of God's creation and family."[45]

The rhetoric of race reconciliation holds that all Christians can join in the building of Christian America. However, it is not a coincidence that in the statement quoted above, Reed does not call for the inclusion of "red" people in the Christian Coalition. The Christian Right is concerned only with reconciling with people of color who are (evangelical) Christian. This Christocentrism has an important impact on which communities of color are included in this "call to unity." As the history of race reconciliation reveals, the Christian Right has focused its efforts primarily on African-Americans. This is because conservative Christians—with the possible exception of the Promise Keepers[46]—tend to define racism as a black-white issue.[47] Conservative Christian articles on race reconciliation

---

dissolved and reformed into the Pentecostal/Charismatic Churches of North America with a 50-50 black-white board. (Stephen Strang, "Unity of Purpose," *Charisma* 20 [January 1995]: 110.) Billy Graham began intensive recruitment of people of color for his Washington Crusade in 1986, his Atlanta crusade in 1994, and his Minneapolis crusade in 1996. (Beth Spring, "Billy Graham's Washington Crusade Gains the Support of Black Church Leaders," *Christianity Today* 30 [13 June 1986]: 10-11; John W. Kennedy, "Deeper than a Handshake," *Christianity Today* 38 [12 December 1994]: 62-63; Ted Olsen, "Lutheran, Catholic, and Black Churches Join Graham Effort," *Christianity Today* 40 [15 July 1996]: 67.) The NAE in its 1994 reorganization announced that it would prioritize combating racism in the church and that it would initiate discussions with the NBEA to cultivate closer relationships. (Timothy Morgan, "NAE Reinvents Itself," *Christianity Today* 38 [4 April 1994]: 87.) *Christianity Today* even went so far as to run a cover story supportive of evangelical Black nationalism. (Wendy Murray Zoba, "Separate and Equal," *Christianity Today* 40 [6 February 1996]: 14-24.)

45Anthony T. Evans, *America's Only Hope* (Chicago: Moody Press, 1990).

46In the New York PK conference, speakers took greater care to address the concerns of non-African-American communities of color than often happens even at more progressive events. *New Man* also regularly runs articles that feature non-African-American men of color and issues particularly pertinent to them. The 1994 PK Clergy conference organizers also apparently made great efforts to include a diversity of men of color. Gayle White, "Clergy Conference Stirs Historic Show of Unity," *Christianity Today* 40 (8 April 1996): 88.

47*Christianity Today* argues that black-white relations are paradigmatic for all other minority relations as blacks have the longest history with U.S. church. (Somehow American Indians escaped their memory.) Consequently, its Institute on Racism only addressed African-Americans. (Andres Tapia, "The Myth of Racial Progress," *Christianity Today* 37 [4 October 1993]: 18 [16-27].) Mark Noll

rarely mention people of color who are not African-American.[48] Of the above-mentioned organizations focusing on race reconciliation, only the Promise Keepers have included non-African-Americans in their program. Addressing racism as an exclusively black-white issue is not limited to the Christian Right. But there may be a reason for the Christian Right's black-white emphasis that is peculiar to the Christian Right. That is, of all communities of color, only African-Americans are judged to be sufficiently "Christian" (that is, Protestant-evangelical) for reconciliation work.

Non-African-American people of color, by contrast, are regarded primarily as objects of mission rather than as partners in reconciliation within the church. Articles on non-African-American people of color tend to fall under titles such as "Foreign Missions: Next Door and Down the Street,"[49] or they describe non-African-American people of color as "the mission field around us."[50] Asian Americans, it seems, have only recently emigrated from "the Heart of Darkness" where the "unseen powers of the demonic realm are noticeably more evident."[51] Somewhat surprisingly, Latinos are only rarely discussed as potential partners in reconciliation.[52] Latinos are still regarded as insufficiently "Christian" because they

---

similarly states, "Black and white divisions are probably the deepest divisions in American religious life." (In J. Lee Grady, "Pentecostals Renounce Racism," 58.) United Evangelical Action's previously mentioned issue on race encompassed only African-Americans. When Christianity Today finally brought together other people of color for one of its institutes, its focus was on "Listening to America's Ethnic Churches," and their evangelism needs. Though all people of color seemed equally concerned about racism, the format did not focus on this issue. Instead the focus was on how these ethnic groups might be "reached."

[48]Phillip Porter, "Take My Hand and Walk with Me," *Charisma* 22 (August 1996): 42-44. This article is typical in that the inset talks about the importance of whites understanding "Minorities," but the article itself talks only about African-Americans.

[49]Don Bjork, "Foreign Missions: Next Door and Down the Street," *Christianity Today* 29 (12 July 1985): 17-21. See also "For Koreans in America, Growth and Growing Pains," *Christianity Today* 33 (3 March 1989): 56.

[50]Richard Pease, "The Mission Field Around Us," *Alliance Witness* 120 (27 February 1985): 20-21. See also Edward Plowman, "Hispanic Christians in the United States," *Christianity Today* 38 (17 January 1996): 44-45.

[51]"South Asia: Into the Heart of Darkness," *Charisma* 18 (January 1993): 27.

[52]Richard Cizik, "The New Conquistadors," *United Evangelical Action* 47 (July–August 1988): 16.

are primarily Roman Catholic. Despite the efforts of the Christian Right to develop coalitions, anti-Catholic sentiment remains strong within a constituency that views Roman Catholicism as the "whore church."[53] Evangelizing U.S. Latinos is also top priority: "If the Hispanics are not reached," says Raimundo Jimenez, "they will be influenced by occultism and by the leftist militants in the universities."[54] The very survival of Los Angeles, he claims, depends upon successful Hispanic mission work. Why? David Neff argues that when Latinos become evangelicals they "no longer participate easily in Latin America's culturally sanctioned corruption; they become honest, industrious, and thrifty; and they resist the tradition of drunkenness."[55] According to Neff, evangelical Latinos are more likely to seek employment and settle happily into U.S. society. Another article claims that upon embracing the "Protestant ethic," Latinos work harder, make more money, and pursue the American dream.[56] These articles reflect a deep-seated belief among members of the Christian Right: Protestantism equals capitalism equals America.[57]

To a degree, what looks like anti-Catholic prejudice is really anti-indigenous prejudice in disguise. That is, Latino Catholics are seen as incomplete Christians because have only partly cast off indigenous traditions; they remain "christo-pagans."[58] Indians tend to be regarded as inassimilable pagans. While evangelicals are at least critical of slavery (even if they overemphasize the role they played in ending the institution), they remain blithely ignorant of the destructiveness of mission work among Indians.[59] They also

---

[53]"Letters," *Cornerstone* 25/108:4.

[54]Dan Wooding, "God's Wake Up Call," *Charisma* 19 (July 1994): 27.

[55]David Neff, "God's Latino Revolution," *Christianity Today* 34 (14 May 1990): 15.

[56]Tapia, "Viva Los Evangelicos!" in "The Myth of Racial Progress," 20.

[57]David Neff, "God's Latino Revolution," *Christianity Today* 34 (14 May 1990): 15.

[58]Chris Woehr, "The Horror of Being a Mexican Evangelical," *Christianity Today* (26 October 1992): 68.

[59]Charles Fiero, "The Ojibwe New Testament: It Sounds Good," *Alliance Life* 123 (23 November 1988): 22-23; Howard G. Hageman, "Colonial Outreach," *The Reformed Journal* 38 (November 1988): 6-7; Lydia Huffman Hoyle, "Elizabeth Morse: Missionary to American Indians," *Baptist History and Heritage* 24 (January 1994): 3-11; Scalberg and Cordell, "A Savage with the Savages," *Moody Monthly*

seem unaware that Indians are largely Christian in some regions. For instance, an article published in 1994 in *Charisma* contends that there is only one church in Tulsa, Oklahoma, that worked with Indians, even though Tulsa supports several Indian churches and most Indians in the city are Christian. The article also states that less than one percent of all Indians are Christians, whereas most statistics place the figure somewhere between twenty-five and fifty percent.[60] *World Christian* describes Indians as "Unreached Peoples," despite decades of enforced attendance in Christian boarding schools.[61] *Moody* still calls Indians "savages."[62] George Jennings denounces even Navajo Christians as under the thrall of "Satan," who continues to "work through cultural features" like peyote.[63] Evangelicals never fully regard Indians as Christian because, as tribal peoples, Indians "continue to be influenced to some degree by the animistic worldview"[64]—in other words, Christian one day, primitive the next.[65] Except as the object of mission work, Native America is almost completely invisible to the Christian Right.

By contrast, African-Americans have finally been "reached" and are now able to partake of the "Christian-American" dream

70 (April 1987): 55-57; Terri Owens, "Breaking the Cycle of Poverty," *World Vision* (October–November 1987): 12-17; "Indians Hold Historic Crusade," *Christianity Today* 32 (17 June 1988): 72.

[60]J. Lee Grady, "America's Forgotten People," *Charisma* 19 (October 1994): 28, 30 (25-32).

[61]Tracy Stewart, "Jesus Walks Among the Navajo," *World Christian* 4 (July/August 1985): 40-41.

[62]Daniel Scalberg and Joy Cordell, "A Savage with the Savages," *Moody Monthly* 70 (April 1987): 55-57. (Interestingly, however, Scalberg and Cordell do admit that the Hurons' conversion to Christianity directly led to their annihilation as a tribe, rendering them unable to cope with the onslaught of the Iroquois.)

[63]George Jennings, "Peyote: Its Appeal to Indian Church Defectors," *Evangelical Missions Quarterly* 26 (January 1990): 64.

[64]Sharon Mumper, "Where in the World Is the Church Growing?" *Christianity Today* (11 July 1986): 21. See also Bob Larson, *Larson's New Book of Cults*, rev. ed. (Wheaton IL: Tyndale, 1989) 106-109; John Ankerberg and John Weldon, *Encyclopedia of New Age Beliefs* (Eugene OR: Harvest House Publishers, 1996) 532-52.

[65]John Maust, "Keeping the Faithful," *Christianity Today* 38 (6 April 1992): 38. See also John Maust, "The Land where Spirits Thrive," *Christianity Today* 29 (13 December 1985): 48-50.

and missionize others.[66] In fact, developing missions work is seen as a sign that a group "has arrived."[67] Testifying to the "successful" conversion of African-Americans to Christianity, *Christianity Today* reported on one African-American church in Oakland, California, that set up a mission in Castro Valley to reach Caucasians.[68] The inclusion of African-Americans within the rhetoric of race reconciliation does not imply a validation of African history or culture: the latter is still viewed as the site of "idol worship and black magic."[69] The Christian Right regards African-Americans as more likely candidates for inclusion, but only to the extent that they are willing to accede to the speciously legitimized account of U.S. Christian imperialism that is touted as "American history" and proclaim, as does John Perkins, that "I am not an African; I am an American. Any black American who puts his allegiance to Africa above his allegiance to America is only hurting himself. . . . United States is my country. I love her."[70]

As mentioned previously, a dominant understanding within the Christian Right is that to be American is to be Christian and to be Christian is to be American. Any history that challenges the Christian basis of America, particularly any history of oppressed groups that challenges U.S. claims to religiomoral superiority, threatens American Christendom itself. As Harold Brown states in his laudatory praise of Columbus: "We cannot repudiate Western civilization and dissociate ourselves from it without at the same time moving ourselves away from Christianity, and potentially

---

[66]Charles Williams, "New Era for Blacks—and Whites," *Alliance Witness* 121 (1 January 1996): 25-26; Leslie Pelt, "Wanted: Black Missionaries, But How?" *Evangelical Missions Quarterly* 25 (January 1989): 28-37; Verne Becker, "A New Era for Black Missionaries," *Christianity Today* 33 (20 October 1989): 38-39.

[67]See J. Alfred Smith, Sr. and Ross Maracle, in "Listening to America's Ethnic Churches," *Christianity Today* 33 (3 March 1989): 32 and 37; John Maust, "Hispanics Eye Mission Role," *Christianity Today* 37 (25 October 1993): 92.

[68]"Man Bites Dog," *Christianity Today* 34 (23 April 1990): 42.

[69]Ron Lee, "Training the World's Evangelists," *Christianity Today* 30 (5 September 1986): 43.

[70]Perkins, "Love Can Build a Bridge," 40, 42 (39-42); see also "Black Magazines Stress Strong Families and Spiritual Values," *Christianity Today* 30 (21 March 1986): 27-28. Says Frank Kent, editor of this new Black magazine, "We are Americans who are Black, not Blacks who are Americans."

from Christ himself."[71] Apparently, for some, Christ is synonymous with Western civilization. Charles Colson, too, complains that "revisionist history" now depicts "Muhammed-inspired Muslims and the pantheistic Native Americans [as] the real good guys." Christians, he suggests, have been falsely implicated in the Spanish Inquisition and the genocide of Indian people. "Take away a sense of history," he warns after tossing history out the window, "and you eviscerate the Christian faith."[72]

Because the maintenance of "Christian-American" history is so important to the Christian Right, the Christian Right will promote race reconciliation and at the same time staunchly oppose any multicultural interpretations of American history.[73] Here may lie the reason the Christian Right ignores Native Americans: any validation of Native society, culture, or religion would call into question the legitimacy of Christian ownership of the land. By contrast, it appears that because African-Americans are viewed by white Christians as safely "Christian" and safely cut off from their African origins, it is now safe for whites to "repent" of their sins of slavery. However, as Indians still have access to their culture and still lay claim to their lands, the Christian Right is not in the same position to "repent" of genocide. Consequently, the forced missionization of Indian people is argued to be a sign of the superiority of white Christians, the only ones willing to "help" others.[74] With few exceptions,[75] the Christian Right strongly supports the heroic myth of Columbus.

Evangelical historian Kay Brigham concedes that there was "a dark [sic] side" to Columbus in that the tribes he "discovered" were decimated. But it is more important that we "admire his

---

[71]Harold O. J. Brown, "The Importance of Being Western," *Christianity Today* 36 (5 October 1992): 46.

[72]Charles Colson, "Dances with Wolves in Sheep's Clothing," *Christianity Today* 36 (27 April 1992): 72. However, a couple of people did write letters complaining about his anti-Indian bias, "Letters," *Christianity Today* 36 (22 June 1992): 11.

[73]Tim Stafford, "Campus Christians and the New Thought Police," *Christianity Today* (19 February 1992): 15-20.

[74]Ibid.

[75]One article that did not celebrate Columbus did so by arguing that he was not a real Christian. Apparently, "Christians" do not commit genocide. "Letters," *Christianity Today* 36 (14 December 1992): 5.

devotion and faith to God."[76] Brigham celebrates this conquest, as well as the expulsion of Jews from Spain, which helped increase the influence of Christ around the world: "I believe God raised up this man to extend the gospel to those religions that had never heard."[77] David Neff concurs that Columbus's role in genocide, his slaveholdings, and his raping of Indian women, are insignificant in light of the fact that he "was motivated by a love for God."[78] While John Eidsmoe admits that Columbus did force Christianity on Native people, "millions of people are in heaven today as a result."[79]

Evangelical/"Assimilationist" Readings

It is very difficult to assimilate Native Americans into this rather narrow Christian-American ideology. Nevertheless, many conservative-evangelical Indians attempt to do so. Such an attempt is represented by an essay written for conservative-evangelical men entitled "The American Indian: The Invisible Man," by Promise Keeper Jeff King (Muscogee). In his essay King indicates his allegiance to America and Christianity. He describes himself as an assimilated child of a military family. He says he does not know his language, and that he was called "white boy" by his Muscogee relatives because his father is white. He calls on all American Indian men to model Christ by forgiving and reconciling with their white Christian brother and to let go of any bitterness incurred by 500 years of genocide.[80]

Yet, this essay indicates the difficulties that even the most "Christian" Indians have in assimilating into Christian America. Even very conservative Christian Indians tend to be clear that

---

[76]Kay Brigham, "The Columbus Nobody Knows," *Christianity Today* 35 (7 October 1991): 27 (26-28). Brigham is quick to falsely assert, however, that these tribes were cannibalistic.

[77]Brigham, "The Columbus Nobody Knows," 28.

[78]David Neff, "The Politics of Remembering," *Christianity Today* 35 (7 October 1991): 29 (28-29).

[79]John Eidsmoe, *Columbus and Cortez, Conquerors for Christ* (Green Forest AR: New Leaf Press, 1992) 140.

[80]Jeff King, "The American Indian: The Invisible Man," in *We Stand Together. Reconciling Men of Different Color*, ed. Rodney Cooper (Chicago: Moody Press, 1995) 80.

Indian nations "have their right to self-government. Whatever power the United States or Canadian governments may exercise over Indian nations is received from the particular tribe or nation—not the other way around."[81]

King similarly charges whites with a biblical mandate to up-hold treaty rights. He disputes traditional white Christian claims to America as a "New Israel," and instead suggests that the proper understanding of America can be found in 2 Samuel where God is depicted as having deserted Saul because he broke his "treaty" with the Gibeonites. Unlike purveyors of the Christian gospel who argue that God will abandon America if America does not continue to uphold biblical principles, King's exegesis implies that God has already abandoned America for its genocidal policies against Indian people. While King discusses the importance of forgiveness, he argues that "wrongs still need to be righted."[82] If Christianity is necessary for salvation, it would seem to justify the missionary conquest of America. Yet, King's essay suggests the opposite:

> Both the public schools and society in general have described America as the promised land to the early settlers, much as Joshua and Israelites properly saw Canaan as the Promised Land. . . . However, in this picture the American Indian was labeled the "heathen," or "savage," much like the enemies of Israel who inhabited the lands they were to occupy based on the promises of God.
>
> Thus, within this erroneous view the taking of the land from these people was justified, and the wrongdoings that were committed were excused. All was interpreted in the light of Manifest Destiny—God designed the land for the pioneers, who were destined to unsettle "savage" Indians from the land.[83]

In another "assimilationist" reading, Rev. Tom Claus, a Mohawk evangelist, stated at a Promise Keepers rally that he

---

[81]Ross Maracle (Mohawk), in "Listening to America's Ethnic Churches," *Christianity Today* 33 (3 March 1989): 36.

[82]Jeff King, "An American Indian Perspective," in *We Stand Together*, ed. Cooper, 95.

[83]Ibid., 82.

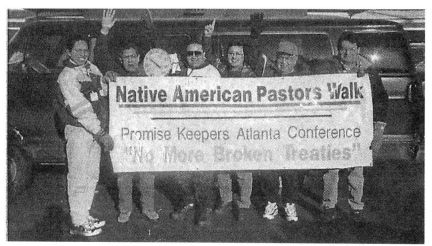

"Native American Pastors Walk," February 1996.

Promise Keepers Clergy Conference, February 1996, Atlanta.
Both photos from *Indian Life* 17/1 (March–April 1996): 9, by permission.

would "rather have Jesus than all the land in the U.S."[84] Frederick Clarkson, a Promise Keeper critic who attended that conference,

---

[84]Quoted in Frederick Clarkson, "Righteous Brothers," *In These Times* 20 (5 August 1996): 16.

noted that the crowd cheered wildly at this comment. I suspect, however, that Clarkson and the crowd misunderstood this comment. Claus likely had no intention of giving up *either* Jesus *or* his land. In fact, in another article, Claus specifically calls evangelicals to lobby their representatives and "express your opposition to those bills which would call for the abrogation of Indian treaties, water, hunting, and fishing rights."[85] At the Promise Keepers clergy conference of 1996, Claus was part of a "No More Broken Promises" walk. In explaining the meaning of this walk, Claus stated that there was "One who did not break his promises. That was Jesus."[86] This statement suggests that, from Claus's perspective, following Jesus is inseparable from respecting Indian land claims. While Claus states this march was not a protest, this statement is an implicit critique of white Christian claims to truth or religious superiority—only Jesus, not Christian missionaries, kept his promises.

Both King and Claus utilize what Jace Weaver terms "communitist" strategies, similar to those strategies used by William Apess and other Indian Christians, involving the turning of the principles of evangelical faith against evangelicals in order to support Native communities.[87] William McLoughlin has similarly noted that the adoption of Christianity does not necessarily connote an allegiance to America. He argues that the many members of the Cherokee Nation converted to Christianity as a means to further the goal of Cherokee nationalism, not of assimilation into "America."[88]

I recall that whenever there was a conflict in translation between the English Bible and the Choctaw Bible in a conservative Southern Baptist, Mississippi Choctaw church I occasionally attended in Chicago, Bible study leaders would unhesitatingly

---

[85]Tom Claus, "Who's Giving What to the Indians?" *United Evangelical Action* 38 (Winter 1979): 26.

[86]"No More Broken Treaties," *Indian Life* 17 (March–April 1996): 8-9.

[87]Jace Weaver. "That the People Might Live: Native Literatures and Communitist Values" (diss., Union Theological Seminary, 1996) 100; subsequently published as *That the People Might Live. Native American Literatures and Native American Community* (New York: Oxford University Press, 1997).

[88]William G. McLoughlin, *Cherokees and Missionaries, 1789–1839*, foreword by William L. Anderson (Norman OK: University of Oklahoma Press, 1995) 335.

state that the Choctaw translation must be the correct one.[89] However, as Joy Anderson notes, "in the United States . . . we find much opposition to the Bible's being in the Indian language. Whites feel Indians should use the English Bible since they can read it."[90] In this church a strong adherence to Christianity and a rejection of Choctaw traditional practices did not translate into an allegiance to white Christians in America. Rather, an adherence to the Choctaw rather than the English Bible signified Choctaw nationalism and a critique of white, English-speaking America.

These readings show the difficulty with the term "assimilation." Even evangelical Indians who refuse to take part in traditional cultural practices may use their Christian identity to resist assimilation into "America." This continued allegiance to Indian nationalism runs directly counter to the political aims of many organizations of the Christian Right groups, which have not only opposed treaty rights in the U.S., but have also financed genocidal campaigns against indigenous people in Latin America.

Indian land rights also tend to run directly counter to the interests of evangelical missions. *Alliance Witness* explicitly states that it is the goal of mission work to stop the Mapuche Indians, who are subject to genocide in Chile, from organizing for land rights or from continuing their cultures, which they call "animism."[91] This fight against Indian sovereignty also provides a subtext for a *World Christian* article on "Jesus Walks among the Navajo." Tracy Stewart notes how "Joe" got saved, and now he has his life together as exemplified by his working for a "coal mining operation on the reservation."[92] Of course, what is not mentioned is the role of coal mining companies, particularly Peabody Coal, in forcing the relocation of the Navajo out of their land in Big Mountain. David Neff argues that while Christians may have stolen Indian land, this "does not require . . . [the] restoration of long-lost lands. (Every

---

[89]Justine Smith, church member, personal conversation.

[90]Joy Anderson, "Reaching Minorities Takes Cultural Acceptance," *Evangelical Missions Quarterly* 24 (July 1988): 242.

[91]Sheryl Ottoson, "Mission to the Mapuches," *Alliance Witness* 19 (18 March 1992): 19.

[92]Stewart, "Jesus Walks among the Navajo," 40.

system of justice knows of a statute of limitations.)"[93] Eidsmoe is not even willing to admit that Christians stole Indian land. He argues that since Native people did not privatize land, and since their communities had not been "established by God," then Europeans had a right to seize the land from them.[94]

The Concerned Women of America was involved in opposing Indian casinos, apparently not because they objected to casinos per se, but because they opposed tribal rather than state control over them.[95] The American Center for Law and Justice, which is supposedly dedicated to "defending and advancing religious liberty," notes that religious liberty does not apply to protecting Indian sacred sites since it is "of immediate interest to only a few Americans."[96] The Christian Coalition also distributed action alerts to its local chapters calling its members to lobby their representatives to eliminate or weaken the Indian Child Welfare Act. Prominent leaders of the Christian Right, such as Robertson, have been active in supporting Latin American regimes that are committing genocide against indigenous people. Former evangelical president of Guatemala, Rios Montt, received much financial support from Pat Robertson which went to fund Rios Montt's Gospel Outreach campaign to annihilate indigenous people. One Gospel Outreach pastor stated: "The Army doesn't massacre the Indians. It massacres demons, and the Indians are demon possessed; they are communists."[97]

Pat Robertson, who has both opposed treaty rights in the U.S. and campaigned against indigenous peoples, notes:

> These tribes are . . . in an arrested state of social development.
> They are not less valuable as human beings because of that, but
> they offer scant wisdom or learning or philosophical vision that

---

[93]David Neff, "The Politics of Remembering," *Christianity Today* 35 (7 October 1991): 29.

[94]Eidsmoe, *Columbus and Cortez, Conquerors for Christ*, 133.

[95]"Field," *Family Voice* 18 (August 1996): 22.

[96]Jay Alan Sekulow, "Religious Freedom Update," *. . . and Nothing But the Truth*, report no. 100 (n.p.: n.d.). (Subsequently published as *And Nothing But the Truth*, by Jay Sekulow and Keith Fournier [Nashville: Thomas Nelson, 1996].)

[97]Quoted by Sara Diamond, *Roads To Dominion: Right-Wing Movements and Political Power in the United States* (New York: Guilford Press, 1995) 238.

can be instructive to a society that can feed the entire population of the earth in a single harvest and send spacecraft to the moon. . . . Except for our crimes, our wars, and our frantic pace of life, what we have is superior to the ways of primitive peoples. . . . Which life do you think people would prefer: freedom in an enlightened Christian civilization or the suffering of subsistence living and superstition in a jungle? *You choose.*[98]

But as the above readings indicate, even "assimilated" Native people, by contrast, are reluctant to equate "enlightened Christian civilization" with the United States.

Traditional/"Oppositional" Readings

The pages of our Bible is all of nature. Our church is the whole world. Our ten commandments are the natural law which is that everything is related.[99]   —Ted Means (Lakota)

Never forget, America is our Hitler.
                    —Chrystos (Menominee) from "Winter Count"[100]

As these quotations indicate, many Native activists, particularly those associated with more radical movements such as the American Indian Movement, reject being defined as either Christian or American. In a sense, they agree more with David Barton's reading of Christian America than with evangelical Native readings. The evangelical readings hold that America does not live up to Christian standards set forth in the Bible and will be judged by them. In the oppositional readings set forth by Native people who advocate a return to traditional religions, they affirm with Barton that America is truly Christian—but that is what is wrong with America. A common story told among Indians is, "When the missionaries came to the Indian, they had the Bible and we had the land. By the time they left, we had the Bible and they had the land." Christianity and America cannot be disentangled; together

---

[98]Pat Robertson, *The Turning Tide* (Dallas: Word Books, 1993) 153.
[99]"Beyond the Pow Wow Conference" (Piscataway Nation), 27 May 1989.
[100]Chrystos. *Dream On* (Vancouver: Press Gang Publishers, 1991).

they represent the genocide of Native people. As George Tinker (Osage) notes in *Missionary Conquest*:

> Europe's colonial conquest of the Americas was largely fought on two separate but symbiotically related fronts. One front was relatively open and explicit; it involved the political and military strategy that drove Indian peoples from their land. . . . The second front, which was just as decisive in the conquest if more subtle and less explicitly apparent, was the religious strategy pursued by missionaries of all denominations. . . . In this conquest . . . theology becomes a crucial ingredient, and the missionaries become an important strategic phalanx.[101]

As Ted Means's statement suggests, oppositional readings often depict Native spirituality as fundamentally distinct from Christianity, including its relationship to the written word. Traditional spirituality is based on orality and community relationships. Its practices are rooted in past traditions but they evolve in relationship to changing contexts. According to such Native traditionalists, Christianity, by contrast, places more importance on faithfulness to the Word of God than to maintaining communal relationships. Christian spirituality, according to many Native people, is mediated through text, whereas traditional spirituality is mediated through interpersonal relationships. They may argue that this importance accorded the written text, and in particular, textual inerrancy, is responsible for the patriarchal and oppressive social structures found in Christian societies, compared to the relatively nonhierarchical and nonpatriarchal social structures found in indigenous communities prior to colonization.[102] As neotraditionalist Russell Means contends:

---

[101]George E. Tinker. *Missionary Conquest. The Gospel and Native American Cultural Genocide* (Minneapolis: Fortress Press, 1993) 120.

[102]See M. Annette Jaimes and Theresa Halsey, "American Indian Women: At the Center of Indigenous Resistance in North America," in *The State of Native America: Genocide, Colonization, and Resistance,* ed. Annette M. Jaimes (Boston: South End Press, 1992) 311-44; and Paula Gunn Allen, *The Sacred Hoop: Recovering the Feminine in American Indian Traditions* (Boston: Beacon Press, 1986; with a new preface, 1992).

I detest writing. The process itself epitomizes the European concept of "legitimate" thinking; what is written has an importance that is denied the spoken. My culture, the Lakota culture, has an oral tradition and so I ordinarily reject writing. It is one of the white world's ways of destroying the cultures of non-European peoples, the imposing of an abstraction over the spoken relationship of a people.[103]

Ironically, while many advocates of Indian traditionalism declare no allegiance to the Written Word in the form of either the Bible or the U.S. Constitution, they often declare their allegiance to another Written Word—Indian treaties. Much of the focus of current Indian organizing attempts to pressure the U.S. government into honoring its treaties with Indian nations. This approach is shared by Indians of all political and spiritual persuasions. Prominent organizations in Indian country include the International Indian Treaty Rights Committee, the Midwest Treaty Network, and a whole host of treaty rights organizations. One of the formative events in contemporary Indian activism has been the Trail of Broken Treaties, a walk across America that led to the Bureau of Indian Affairs building takeover in 1972. The basis of this march was a call to reopen the treaty-making process and to call attention to the history of broken treaties in U.S. history.[104] While many Indian nationalists abhor biblical inerrancy, they often supplant it with Treaty inerrancy. Indian treaties are the supreme law of the land—they must be followed strictly. Just as David Barton opposes legal scholars who wish to adapt the Constitution to today's context, Indian nationalists oppose the efforts of white antitreaty organizations, such as Stop Treaty Abuse, who want to "modernize" the treaties by adapting them to the contemporary situation.[105]

Evangelical Indians attempt to hold "America" to biblical standards. Indian traditionalists, by contrast, attempt to hold

---

[103]Russell Means, "The Same Old Song," in *Marxism and Native Americans*, ed. Ward Churchill (Boston: South End Press, 1983) 19.

[104]See Vine Deloria, Jr., *Behind the Trail of Broken Treaties: An Indian Declaration of Independence* (Austin: Univ. of Texas Press, 1985; orig.: New York: Dell, 1974).

[105]See Rick Whaley and Walter Bresette, *Walleye Warriors: An Effective Alliance against Racism and for the Earth* (Philadelphia: New Society Publishers, 1994) 17-21.

"America" to treaty standards. However, just as maintaining the legitimacy of biblical standards in a sense legitimizes a non-Indian framework as paradigmatic for Indians, upholding the treaties as foundational legitimizes the U.S. takeover of Indian land. By arguing that the treaties are the "supreme law of the land" in order to protect Indians from multinational corporations that want to take over what little Indian land is left, Native peoples are then forced to concede that the treaties legitimately transfer the great majority of Indian land to white people. What remains unquestioned is the illegitimate manner in which these treaties were imposed upon Native nations. While denying their "Americaness," many traditionals implicitly recognize a fundamental relationship to the U.S. in the form of treaty relations.

It is this paradigm that Chrystos rejects in her poem: "I Have Not Signed a Treaty with the U.S. Government."[106] She declares that Indian people have given up no land to the U.S. government—that the U.S. government is completely null and void. She does not respect the written text that treaties signify. Rather the treaties are nothing more than "old sorry paper." Furthermore, she nullifies this "old sorry paper" through her spoken word. She declares that the U.S. government should take "these words" back home with it. And of course, many Native people reject the paradigm in theory, but in practical terms see no other way to resist corporate encroachment on Indian lands other than through the rhetoric of treaty rights.

In declaring that there is no treaty, Chrystos is also declaring that there is no relationship between the U.S. and Indian nations. The U.S. is "nobody we know." The U.S. has "no children no elders no relatives." The poem echoes Russell Means's sentiment that the written word displaces human relationships when Chrystos declares that in the U.S, "No one lives in the houses but paper." Relationship has been replaced by paper—the written word.

The irony that such a poem is in written form is not lost upon Native people. Nor do Native people ignore the tragedy that many traditional people, such as Russell Means, are forced to advocate

---

[106]Chrystos. *Not Vanishing* (Vancouver: Press Gang Publishers, 1988) 71.

the primacy of oral tradition in the English language rather than in their tribal tongue. The title of poet Joy Harjo's (Muscogee) book, *Reinventing the Enemy's Language*, illustrates these tensions. As Laura Donaldson notes in her discussion of writing as a colonial technology, American Indians are trapped in an evil dualism in discourses about literacy: literacy either "saves" them from savagery or condemns them to cultural alienation and loss. This binary "fails to ask how formerly oral societies, 'far from being passively transformed by literacy, instead actively and creatively apply literate skills to suit their own purposes and needs.' "[107] Consequently, some Native writer/activists explore issues of Christian and American identities that see alternatives to these binaries. I will explore such an approach in the final section of this paper.

Part 3
Decentering Christian America—An Indigenous Proposal

Vine Deloria notes that neotraditionalist attempts to reclaim Native spirituality often draw upon an either/or system of logic (that is, Christian versus traditional; American versus Indian; oral versus written) that is foreign to Native cultures.[108] According to the European positivist grammar of truth, if proposition *p* is true, then *not-p* must be false. Indigenous epistemologies are not beholden to such logic systems. Beliefs, even systems of belief, that seem contradictory to European and Euro-American culture—for example, Christianity and indigenous religions—can coexist in indigenous cultures. For example, at a conference several years ago I heard a story about an Indian man who gave a speech in which he claimed that the next speaker was going to say things that were completely wrong. When his turn came, the next speaker, also Indian, began not by attacking the preceding speaker, but by

---

[107]Laura Donaldson, "Writing the Talking Stick: Alphabetic Literacy as Colonial Technology and Postcolonial Appropriation," unpublished paper, 3.

[108]Vine Deloria, "A Native American Perspective on Liberation," *Occasional Bulletin of Missionary Research* 1 (July 1977): 17. Ironically, however, Deloria himself maintains in an either/or fashion: "We cannot reject the Christian religion piecemeal . . . the whole religion has been misdirected from its inception." In his *God Is Red: A Native View of Religion* (Golden CO: North American Press, 1992) 265.

announcing that everything the previous speaker had said was completely true! The event is notable because it struck no one present—not the speakers, not the Indian audience—as odd.

As a consequence, some Native writers seek not so much to displace the myths of Christian America, but to decenter them from their hegemonic positions. I will focus on one such work, Thomas King's *Green Grass, Running Water*. King's reading of Christian America follows what Charles Mabee describes as processes of "regionalization" and "differentiation."[109] That is, King decenters the biblical myth of "Christian America" by regionalizing it—situating it in time and place—thus calling into question its claims of universality. It further "differentiates" the myth by placing it in dialogue with Native myths. Whereas in the dominant culture, Native myths are often "read" into the hegemonic myth of Christian America (that is, Native people are the children of Shem), in *Green Grass, Running Water*, Christian America/Canada is read into Native myths of origin.

Religion scholar Wesley Kort notes that one of staple beliefs of contemporary American culture is that "we live without the assistance of culture, encounter reality directly, and see things as they really are. Unlike other peoples and people of former centuries, we live in *the* world and not in *a* world, in the world as it *actually is*."[110] *Green Grass, Running Water*, in contrast, attempts to delineate *a* world that Christian America lives in. King begins: "So. In the beginning, there was nothing. Just the water."[111] The first part of this line refers to common Christian understandings of creation *ex nihilo*. Native stories of origin, however, generally do not describe creation *ex nihilo*; they tell the origins of a particular tribe and how it came to be in a particular place—they describe how *a* world, not *the* world, was created. King subverts the universal *ex nihilo* narrative by hedging it with the phrase, "Just the water," and in

---

[109]Charles Mabee, *Reimagining America: A Theological Critique of the American Mythos and Biblical Hermeneutics*, StABH 1 (Macon GA: Mercer University Press, 1985) 103, 104.

[110]Wesley Kort, *"Take, Read": Scripture, textuality, and Cultural Practice* (University Park PA: Pennsylvania State University Press, 1996) 10.

[111]Thomas King, *Green Grass, Running Water* (New York: Bantam, 1993) 1.

doing so, "regionalizes" Christian myths within their particular cultural context.

Not only does *Green Grass, Running Water* reject the foundational importance of Christian myths of origin; it attempts to regionalize the Christian God by recasting God as a creation of the Indian trickster, Coyote. Coyote has a dream that becomes so self-important that it begins to believe it is in charge of the world. Coyote tells the dream that it can be a "dog," but the dream gets its name backwards and thinks it is "god." This dream then complains: "But why am I a little god?"[112] Coyote grants the dream its wish and it becomes G O D. Coyote later dreams up the Garden of Eden, in which Ah-Damn, Coyote, and First Woman begin feasting on the food. G O D then appears on the scene.

> I'm G O D, says G O D. And I am almost as good as Coyote.
> Funny, says First Woman, You remind me of a dog.
> And just so we keep things straight, says that G O D, this is my world and this my garden.
> Your garden, says First Woman. You must be dreaming. . . .
> Anybody who eats my stuff is going to be very sorry, says that G O D. There are rules, you know . . . Christian Rules.[113]

King's retelling of the Genesis story textualizes both G O D and G O D's commandments and undercuts Christianity's pretense to a universal discourse on morality and creation.

King's G O D is not only a creation rather than a creator, it is a creation of Coyote. We later learn that Coyote's antics lead to both the birth of Christ and the Great Flood. As a trickster, Coyote represents a creative but unpredictable force whose power often wreaks havoc on the world:

> The trickster is a rebel against authority and the breaker of all taboos. He is what the best-behaved and most circumspect person may secretly wish to be. He is . . . at the same time imp and hero . . . who can make mischief beyond belief. . . . In an

---

[112]Ibid., 2.
[113]Ibid., 2.

ordered world . . . he represents the potency of nothingness, of chaos, of freedom.[114]

Chaos occurs when creatures, including human beings, lose sense of their place in the world—that is, when they forget that they are related to all of creation and that their actions affect everyone and everything else. Native people often refer to all aspects of creation (the land, the air, the water, the animals . . .) as "all my relatives" in order to signal the importance of understanding the fundamental interconnectedness of all things. The trickster's chaotic actions may disrupt cosmic harmony, but they also render new possibilities. In *Green Grass, Running Water*, the Christian G O D represents a creation of the trickster that does create something new, but it unfortunately loses its perspective and disrupts the world's balance. It forgets who created it, and begins to think it is all-powerful and accountable to no one. G O D forgets its relatives.

The problem with the Christian myth, according to King, is the arrogance of its presumption to universality. This arrogance is reflected in the following interchange between Young Man Walking on Water, a.k.a. Jesus, and Old Woman.

> I [Young Man Walking on Water] am now going to walk across the water to that vessel. I am going to calm the seas and stop all the agitation. . . .
> So Young Man Walking on Water walks on the water to that Boat. With those men.
> Help us! Help us! say those men. . . .
> Stop rocking! He says to the Boat. Stop rocking!
> But those Waves keep getting higher, and that Boat keeps rocking.
> Help us! Say those men. Help us!
> Whee, say those happy Waves.
> Calm down! Stop rocking! Calm down! Stop rocking, says Young Man Walking on Water.
> But that doesn't happen, and those men on that Boat begin to throw up.
> Yuck, says that Boat. Now look what happened.

---

[114]Richard Erdoes and Alfonso Ortiz, eds., *American Indian Myths and Legends* (New York: Pantheon, 1984) 335.

Well, Old Woman watches Young Man Walking on Water.
. . . Pardon me, she says, Would you like some help.

There you go again, says Young Man Walking on Water.
Trying to tell me what to do.

Well, says Old Woman, someone has to. You are acting as
though you have no relations. You shouldn't yell at those happy
Waves. You shouldn't shout at that jolly Boat. You got to sing a
song. . . . It's simple song, says Old Woman. And Old woman
sings her song. . . .

Boy, says those Waves, that is one beautiful song. We feel
real relaxed.

Yes, says that Boat, it sure is. Maybe I'll take a nap.

So the Boat stops rocking, and those Waves stop rising higher
and higher, and everything calms down.

Hooray, say those men. We are saved.

Hooray, says young Man Walking on Water. I have saved
you.

Actually, says those men, that other person saved us.

Nonsense, says Young Man Walking on Water. That other
person is a woman. . . .

By golly, says those men. Young Man Walking on Water
must have saved us after all. We better follow him around.[115]

In a sense G O D and Young Man Walking on Water serve as
critique not only of the destructive power of a particular exclusive
and hegemonic worldview, but also of attempts to replace one
such exclusive worldview with another, including Indian nationalism. King offers not one but four origin stories from Indian perspectives; no single story seeks to replace the Christian myth.
King's novel highlights what Mabee calls differentiation—the referencing of one's claims to truth by way of other claims to truth.
Native people might call this process relationality—recognizing
how one's story is related to other stories and respecting the
integrity of those stories.

Coyote is accompanied through the novel by four Indians—the
Lone Ranger, Hawkeye, Ishmael, and Robinson Crusoe—who
attempt to straighten out the mess Coyote made by inadvertently
creating G O D and, consequently, Christian North America. They

---

[115]King, *Green Grass, Running Water*, 389-91.

intervene in the lives of a Blackfoot family who are resisting an impending dam project on their land. At the same time, they flow in and out of religious, literary, and pop-cultural myths of America—from John Wayne movies, to the Garden of Eden, to Moby Dick. At the end of the novel, they end up "in the beginning" again. These characters are able to correct some of Coyote's damage—for instance, they alter a John Wayne movie so that the Indians win a shoot-out. However, their changes always come undone, forcing them to begin again their attempts to restore cosmic balance.

King's sense of time directly challenges Christian understandings of linear time in which Creation is inexorably headed toward the final day of judgement. Rather, time in King's novel is cyclical: whatever is accomplished eventually falls apart and must be restored. Cosmic balance is never achieved "once and for all." It has no final goal in the sense that Jesus' resurrection promises final redemption. It requires constant maintenance.

King's narrative also serves as a rebuke to Blonsky and Bloom's descriptions of America. Whereas Bloom and Blonsky envision "America" as something imposed upon outsiders—for example, American Indians—King's "America" is in fact created by Indian mythology. The American figures of Robinson Crusoe, Hawkeye, Ishmael, and the Lone Ranger, are Indians. Gerald Vizenor takes a similar line in his *Heirs of Columbus*, a story in which a part-Native Columbus, the descendant of Mayans who had "discovered" Europe centuries before, sets sail for "home." Native characters in these counterstories actually have a hand in creating America, even as they resist its encroachments upon Native traditions.

As Vine Deloria notes, "most tribal religions make no pretense as to their universality or exclusiveness. They integrate the respective communities as particular people chosen for particular religious knowledge and experiences."[116] Without doubt, such a pragmatic worldview prevents many Native people from making universalist claims about spirituality or liberation; however, it also suggests that no other discourse, including Christian discourse in any of its manifestations, is in a position to do so either. This

---

[116]Deloria, *God Is Red*, 210.

understanding is reflected in King's project. King does not propose an alternative Truth to supplant Christian-American discourse; rather, he regionalizes and differentiates Christian-American mythology by placing it in the varied contexts of Native stories.

Conclusion

The reading of Christian America and the Bible suggested by Thomas King is not a complete answer to the Christian Right's reading of the Bible for Native people. While I have shown that oppositional readings to Christian America often implicitly uphold what they try to deconstruct, such readings may in certain cases be strategically necessary. For instance, the rhetoric of opposition, while perhaps more simplistic than the approach taken by King, may be more effective in politicizing Indians to fight for their survival. Given the power imbalances between Native communities and the dominant culture, Native people have had to fight for survival with any tools at their disposal.

I have shown that the Christian Right is not monolithic and that its very own doctrines, particularly biblical inerrancy, while seeming to reify its conservative political positions in some sectors, actually calls into question these positions in other sectors. The Christian Right's Christian America thus contains the seeds of its own deconstruction. Furthermore, biblicism, when utilized by resistant communities such as American Indians, can further the destabilization of Christian America. Thus, even seemingly "assimilationist" readings can be politically effective in resisting the Christian Right.

Contrary to the popular maxim, sometimes the master's tools *can* dismantle the master's house. However, Thomas King's approach of reading Christian America represents a resistant reading to Christian America that acknowledges the pervasive impact of Christian colonization on Indian people. It allows Indian people to see themselves not just as victims of America who either oppose it or assimilate into it, but as people who actively take part in creating America even as they disown it. Contrary to Mabee's claim that American Indians "could not share the American myth,"[117] it is evident that not only *have* Indians shared in the myth, but the American myth itself could not exist without them.

---

[117]Charles Mabee. *Reading Sacred Texts through American Eyes: Biblical Interpretation as Cultural Critique,* StABH 7 (Macon GA: Mercer University Press, 1991) 14.

"It's a Small World . . . " Abraham Lincoln, the New American Myth, and the Biblical Rhetoric of Unity

Harold Rhee

President Abraham Lincoln's construction of the American myth was based partly upon a certain reading of the Bible, a reading that focused on forgiveness, ethical sensitivity to one's neighbor, and reconciliation. Lincoln attempted to construct the prototypical, ideal American to be a loving creature, not one who would willingly fight against another American. America was to be a land of conflict resolution, not of Civil War. Difference was to disappear, and an American identity based upon biblical values was to be common for all Americans. Lincoln's rhetoric, oddly enough, was a rhetoric of unity and love. This dimension of the American myth exists to this day, even and especially in such seemingly innocent places as recreational tourist attractions. Walt Disney World is a famous example. Through an analysis of Lincoln's Second Inaugural Address and the Walt Disney World attraction "It's a Small World," I hope to identify some of the common characteristics of American mythologies, especially those drawn from the Bible.

"It's a Small World . . . "

In the spring of 1997, I spent some time at Walt Disney World in Orlando, Florida with my family. I had been there once before about twenty years ago, and was interested in finding out what I remembered. Suddenly, I flashed back to my childhood fear of roller coasters, the boredom of waiting in long lines, and the only attraction I remembered—"It's a Small World." It is this attraction that provoked my interest in Abraham Lincoln in connection with the American myth.

I remembered "It's a Small World" to be a simple ride, but after riding it a second time as an adult, it did not seem so simple after all. In seven minutes, riding a mechanical boat, I learned what everybody in this small world of ours looked like. I learned that we all wore different clothes, ate different foods, and had different ways of life. At the same time, I learned how similar we all were. Through the magic of Disney, every human representation became a three-foot-tall mechanical figure, with a perpetual smile on each face, singing in rhythm (and in perfect English, no less!) the words of the theme song:

> It's a small world, after all;
> it's a small world, after all;
> it's a small world, after all;
> it's a small, small world.[1]

I was not sure whether I was in heaven or in hell. Everyone seemed so happy and got along with each other so well. I figured, I must be in hell because I was participating in a recurring American myth, a myth which had the rhetoric of unity as its basis. Difference and conflict became decorations and ornaments in that myth. Walt Disney World removed the threat and conflict that difference had always posed for America. The Japanese kimono, the African tribal ceremony, and the Spanish fiesta—these looked like parts of a children's make-believe game, rather than representations of cultural identities. Smiles, hugs, and kisses were treated with an almost religious orthodoxy. Happiness was the norm. The complexity of world history was reduced to the level of a children's cartoon.

The history of "It's a Small World" sheds some light on the ideology behind this ride:

---

[1]From *It's a Small World*, by Richard M. Sherman and Robert B. Sherman (©1963).

Always a front runner in new technology, Disney opened four exhibits at the New York World's Fair in 1964. . . . Pepsi-Cola supported It's a Small World, an exhibit established to promote UNICEF, a United Nations child welfare organization; it consisted of mechanized children from all over the world dressed in their native costumes and promoting world peace. The most ambitious of the World's Fair projects, funded by the World's Fair Committee, introduced an Audio-Animatronics® Abraham Lincoln."[2]

This statement reveals much. It was made in response to a World's Fair, and most likely in response to the Vietnam War.[3] And, ironically, this ride was made in conjunction with an Abraham Lincoln presentation, possibly to commemorate the centennial of the end of the Civil War and Lincoln's subsequent assassination. Because of Lincoln's reputation as a peacemaker, the focus upon Abraham Lincoln was deemed quite appropriate in relationship to the "It's a Small World" ideology.

However, I would also like to expand on what was meant by "native costumes." Disney's interpretation of what was "native" came out of a Western European social-scientific construct which Edward Said calls "Orientalism." In this construct, the Orient, including Africa and Asia, was seen as a myth often isolated from any consideration of actual history or current reality:

In a sense Orientalism was a library or archive of information commonly and, in some of its aspects, unanimously held. . . . they allowed Europeans to deal with and even to see Orientals as a phenomenon possessing regular characteristics.[4]

This assumed that "real" Orientals did not possess regular characteristics. Orientalism attempted to remove, or at least to distance, the threat that the Orient symbolized for Western Europe.

---

[2]Kathy M. Jackson, *Walt Disney: a Bio-Bibliography* (Westport CT: Greenwood, 1993) 64-65.

[3]Comment made by Ann Herpel during Prof. Vincent Wimbush's class, "The Bible and (De)Construction of the American Myth," Union Theological Seminary, New York, 24 April 1997.

[4]Edward Said, *Orientalism* (New York: Vintage Books, 1978) 41-42.

Biblical Studies was the first field that studied the Orient in the manner Said describes.[5] Europeans, and in recent years especially Americans, dominate the scholarly study of the Bible. Ironically, scholars from the Middle East are not as influential and are sometimes ignored altogether, even though they are arguably closer culturally and geographically to the Bible than Europeans or Americans. This says much about the agenda of Orientalism—to study a foreign area in a way that supports, and even benefits, European and American cultural superiority:

> This is obviously true of the literary pilgrims, beginning with Chateaubriand, who found in the Orient a locale sympathetic to their private myths, obsessions, and requirements. Here we notice how all the pilgrims . . . exploit the Orient in their work so as in some urgent way to justify their existential vocation.[6]

If one can go beyond the naive notion of Biblical Studies as a study purely of religion, faith, and God, or as study of specific ancient historical periods, one would then be able to see Biblical Studies as a practice of intellectual mythmaking and epistemological colonialism.

Just as Walt Disney World is not interested in what this small world *really* looks like, but instead, what some Americans would *hope* this world would look like, many European and American biblical scholars have seemed to be interested in the "truth" only to the extent that it squares with the overarching mythologies of their own cultures. When the "Orient" is studied, it is in a way which displaces the Oriental, and affirms the Occidental.[7] The corporation that is behind Walt Disney World, Abraham Lincoln, and many foundationalist biblical scholars are all engaged in the similar activity of *re*-membering and *re*-constructing the past. They are not interested in the objective *re*-collection of the past. Their work, which displaces the "other" and replaces it with the dominant cul-

---

[5]Ibid., 51.

[6]Ibid., 170.

[7]"To speak of scholarly specialization as a geographical 'field' is, in the case of Orientalism, fairly revealing since no one is likely to imagine a field symmetrical to it called Occidentalism." Ibid., 50.

tural norms, has a profound impact on the study of the strategies of culture formation.

President Lincoln at the "Great Moments with Mr. Lincoln" attraction at Disneyland® Park. Copyright ©Disney Enterprises, Inc.

Within the "Small World," "native" becomes a very romanticized ideal. Asian children wear Asian dress such as kimonos and saris, even though many natives no longer wear such clothes. Africans are presented in a setting filled with large, exotic plants and animals, an obvious reference to primitivism, without any reference to present-day Africans. So, in other words, the Disney notion of peace is based upon a return to "historical" notions of foreign cultures. Every culture is simultaneously made intimate and non-threatening through the use of children, and made foreign and mysterious through the use of stereotypes based on colonial myths.

Nevertheless, "It's a Small World" acts as a manifesto for world peace. To believe in the Disney myth is to believe in world peace and unity. At least, that is what Disney may have intended with this attraction.

Lincoln's Second Inaugural Address

How does Abraham Lincoln fit into all this? Despite the fact that in the Civil War people were killing each other daily, and communities were being ransacked and destroyed, Abraham Lincoln created an imaginary world quite similar to a Walt Disney World attraction. In his American myth, differences and pluralism were ignored. It did not matter what your stance on slavery was, or whether you fought for the Union or the Confederacy, you were an American, and in order to be true to your American identity, you had to love the other. In other words, you had to learn to ignore difference. The Civil War was thought of as a divine test to see how far Americans would go to love one another, even in the aftermath of a war. As Lincoln wrote in his Second Inaugural Address, "The Almighty has His own purposes. . . . He gives to both North and South this terrible war as the woe due to those by whom the offense came."[8]

This comparison of Lincoln to Disney does not treat the Civil War, or Abraham Lincoln, lightly. But in order to understand how Lincoln to a certain degree succeeded in bringing America back together after the Civil War, one must take seriously the construction and function of myth. To do that, one must begin to understand how the American imagination was exercised in an effort to find peace, justice, and liberty in the midst of war, death, and slavery. In institutions such as the American presidency, Walt Disney World, and the church, our imaginations are stretched in the face of traumatic events. Whether it is cultural, racial, sexual, or religious conflict, difference is ignored or devalued in the name of unity.

---

[8]"Second Inaugural Address (4 March 1865)," in *The Life and Writings of Abraham Lincoln*, ed. P. V. D. Stern (New York: Modern Library, 1940) 842.

The Second Inaugural Address[9] was given on 4 March 1865, roughly four weeks before General Lee's surrender to General Grant at Appomattox Courthouse, and five weeks before the assassination of Lincoln by John Wilkes Booth in Washington D.C. As Lincoln himself mentioned, it was a short address: "At this second appearing to take the oath of the presidential office there is less occasion for an extended address than there was at the first."[10]

The first half of the address was general background to the start of the war. Although Lincoln mentioned that "a statement somewhat in detail . . . seemed fitting and proper,"[11] what was notable about the first half of the address was its discussion of the war in highly abstract terms. It did not name people, nor did it identify the Confederacy by name. He used the term "insurgent" to refer to the Confederacy: "insurgent agents were in the city seeking to destroy it without war."[12] This vagueness of language was the beginning of Lincoln's rhetoric of unity. He avoided any language that might identify any community as different, because difference was what had caused the conflict in the first place.

In the following paragraph, Lincoln discussed the role of slavery in the Civil War, referring to the slaves as an "interest": "These slaves constituted a peculiar and powerful interest. All knew that this interest was, somehow, the cause of the war."[13] Once again, the description veered towards abstraction—it is difficult to identify exactly what was the relationship between slavery and the Civil War. Once again, his discussion avoided any concrete reference to pluralism and difference. Below, I shall analyze Lincoln's discussion to show why his construction of the American myth had to avoid the issue of the slaves altogether.

"Both read the same Bible and pray to the same God, and each invokes His aid against the other. . . . the prayers of both could not be answered."[14] Lincoln acknowledged that there was a conflict. But just as everyone at Walt Disney World was a three-foot-tall

---

[9]Ibid., 839-42.
[10]Ibid., 840.
[11]Ibid.
[12]Ibid., 841.
[13]Ibid.
[14]Ibid.

wooden figure, Lincoln emphasized commonality and sameness over difference: "Both read the *same* Bible and pray to the *same* God" (my emphasis). As James Silver and Mark Noll document, much of Civil War America interpreted the Bible as a document advocating holy war.[15] As Noll writes, "Southerners excelled in this exercise. Lincoln was Pharaoh; Jefferson Davis, Moses; and Yankees in general, Judas."[16] Yet Lincoln interpreted the Bible as a document teaching unity, forgiveness, and charity. From this point on, Lincoln turned to the Bible in a full-scale construction and production of his new American myth.

Biblical References in the Second Inaugural Address

Lincoln's Second Inaugural Address is filled with biblical references. As William Wolf says, "It reads like a supplement to the Bible."[17] There are some word-for-word quotations, and some references to a phrase or word from the Bible (King James Version). Examples of full quotations Lincoln used, sometimes in altered form, are Genesis 3:19, "bread from the sweat of other men" (original reads, "in the sweat of thy face shalt thou eat bread"); Matthew 7:1, "let us judge not, that we be not judged"; Matthew 18:7, "Woe unto the world because of offenses; for it must needs be that offenses come, but woe to that man by whom the offense cometh"; and Psalm 19:9, "the judgments of the Lord are true and righteous altogether."[18]

Examples of phrases or words from the Bible include: "To care for . . . his widow and his orphan,"[19] taken from various passages in Deuteronomy and Isaiah. In quoting Deuteronomy 26:12, "and has given it unto the Levite, the stranger, the fatherless, and the widow . . . ," Lincoln keeps the reference to the widow and the

---

[15]James W. Silver, *Confederate Morale and Church Propaganda* (Tuscaloosa AL: Confederate Publishing, 1957) 25-26.

[16]Mark A. Noll, "The Image of the U.S. as a Biblical Nation, 1776–1865," in *The Bible in America: Essays in Cultural History*, ed. Nathan Hatch and Mark Noll (New York: Oxford University Press, 1982) 44.

[17]William J. Wolf, *The Religion of Abraham Lincoln* (New York: Seabury, 1963) 136.

[18]"Second Inaugural Address," 841-42.

[19]Ibid., 841.

orphan and removes the reference to the Levite and the stranger. The reference to the Civil War as a "mighty *scourge* of war"[20] may refer to passages in the Passion narrative of Jesus in the gospels (for example, Matthew 27:26, "but Jesus he scourged and delivered to be crucified").

In addition, the reference to the "lash" may be compared to the smiting of Jesus on the head with a reed (Matthew 27:30). And "paid by another drawn with the sword," could be a reference to the appearances of angels with drawn swords during the many wars in the Old Testament, such as Joshua 5:13. The phrase, "With malice toward none," could be a vague reference to 1 Peter 2:1; and "charity for all" seems to be a reference to 1 Corinthians 13 (the King James Version sometimes translates *agape* as "charity").[21]

The majority of these references are from passages that emphasize the condemnation of violence or unethical behavior, the resolution of conflict, and the necessity to care for others. This lent biblical support for Lincoln's belief that the Civil War was something that must quickly be put to an end and that Americans should reconcile because it was the proper, that is, the biblical, way to be Americans. The Bible, as Lincoln interpreted it, was a text of love and unity, not of war.

Identifying Lincoln's Rhetoric

Charles Mabee's analysis of Benjamin Franklin describes the dilemma America has faced since colonization:

Franklin produces a foretaste for perhaps the single most important theological issue to result from the experience of American pluralism: how can any single dogmatic viewpoint be advanced by a given tradition within a pluralistic religious environment? Unless that tradition accepts a certain degree of relativity in its convictions, it finds itself splintered off from the others in an unhealthy posture of self-defense. . . . Of course, the other side of the coin is that one's religious tradition may venture too far in the direction of relativity, blandly affirming that all traditions are

---

[20]Ibid.
[21]All quotations, ibid., 841.

equally true. Franklin correctly saw this great problem of American public religion.[22]

For Lincoln, the problem of pluralism and difference was very serious, because the Civil War was the result of a pluralistic society that had not been kept in check. Differing opinions on slavery had grown into differing opinions regarding God's destiny for America. Did God want America to be slave or free?[23] The cultural divide between North and South was growing larger and larger. Before the Civil War, a general and vague sense of official American identity was enough to keep the country together, but now two different American identities were forming. The mythic spin notwithstanding, America had always been made up of a collection of different identities—different political groups, different religions, different denominations, different ways-of-life, different racial and ethnic groups—and tension had always existed among these different identities. But now the tension became irreconcilable, and only the Civil War could resolve it, or exacerbate it.

Lincoln always viewed the Bible as something that could help overcome or at least bridge the differences. This may be related to his negative experience with the divisiveness of Christian denominations he had witnessed at an earlier age.[24] As Lincoln saw it, too many American Christians argued vigorously over which church had the best doctrine of predestination, what the pros and cons of slavery were, and who was to win the Civil War. These arguments were set in the context of biblical interpretation. These and other arguments were set in the context of biblical interpretation that was inspired by different, conflicting motives:

---

[22]Charles Mabee, *Reimagining America: A Theological Critique of the American Mythos and Biblical Hermeneutics*, StABH 7 (Macon GA: Mercer University Press, 1985) 60.

[23]Silver, *Confederate Morale and Church Propaganda* 25-26.

[24]"What must have disturbed [Lincoln] still more was the violent feuding between the jealous denominations. One form of Baptist predestinarian opinion held that its church members were created by God for heaven whereas the greater part of mankind had been destined for eternal flames. Methodists and Baptists denounced each other on whether the road to heaven passed over dry land or water. . . . [T]he bitterness of sectarian prejudice must have been repellent to him, and was probably a cause of his lasting reluctance to affiliate with any sect." Wolf, *The Religion of Abraham Lincoln*, 41-42.

> Did ministers, preaching from the Bible as public spokesmen [*sic*], really use Scripture as a primary source for the convictions they expressed? Or did they in fact merely exploit Scripture to sanctify convictions—whether nationalistic, political, social or racial—which had little to do with biblical themes?[25]

It is arguable that up to the time of the Civil War in the U.S., and throughout the history of its use, the Bible had been used generally to emphasize and sharpen differences and legitimize the superiority of the one viewpoint over competing ones. Yet, Lincoln used the Bible to show commonality, charity, humility before God, and forgiveness. The Bible provided the rhetorics with which he could communicate to America what his vision of American identity and destiny should be based upon. He presented the possibility of a mythical land where there was, "malice toward none; with charity for all."[26]

For Lincoln, survival and maintenance of the Union was always his primary goal:

> I would save the Union. I would save it the shortest way under the Constitution. . . . If there be those who would not save the Union, unless they could at the same time *save* slavery, I do not agree with them. If there be those who would not save the Union unless they could at the same time *destroy* slavery, I do not agree with them. My paramount object in this struggle is to save the Union, and is *not* either to save or to destroy slavery.[27]

The emancipation of the slaves became important to him only when he realized how effective an Emancipation Proclamation would be on Union morale.[28] But even then Lincoln did not focus on the destruction of the institution of slavery in his address. Instead, he focused on slavery as it related to American unity and identity:

---

[25]Noll, "The Image of the U.S. as a Biblical Nation, 1776–1865," 41.

[26]"Second Inaugural Address," 842.

[27]"Letter to Horace Greeley (August 22, 1862)," in *The Life and Writings of Abraham Lincoln*, 718-19.

[28]James O. Robertson, *American Myth, American Reality* (New York: Hill & Wang, 1980) 89.

These slaves constituted a peculiar and powerful interest. All knew that this interest was, somehow, the cause of the war. To strengthen, perpetuate, and extend this interest was the object for which the insurgents would rend the Union, even by war; while the government claimed no right to do more than to restrict the territorial enlargement of it.[29]

Lincoln presented slavery as a cause of the war, but instead of presenting the slaves as active agents of the war, the slaves were a silent and "peculiar" interest that provoked the "insurgents" and the "Government" to fight.[30] The conflict that he tried to resolve was not the moral issue of slavery, but the political issue of national unity, cast in moral terms. In his construction of the new American myth, the slave (including the freed slave) was not included, especially in light of Lincoln's opinion that black equality would never be achieved.[31]

For both Presidents Lincoln and Jefferson Davis national identity was viewed as a moral issue. An example is the many decrees calling for days of fasting during the Civil War. Jefferson Davis called for nine national days of fasting; Lincoln called for four.[32] For Lincoln, this was seen as a time for prayer and humiliation:

We have been the recipients of the choicest bounties of Heaven. We have been preserved, these many years, in peace and prosperity. We have grown in numbers, wealth, and power as no other nation has ever grown. But we have forgotten God.[33]

---

[29]"Second Inaugural Address," 841.

[30]Ibid.

[31]"More than most Americans of his time, [Lincoln] realized the implications and the enormous difficulties of black equality." Robertson, *American Myth, American Reality*, 89.

Also, Lincoln says, in speaking to a group of African Americans regarding moving to a new country or colony, "The aspiration of men is to enjoy equality with the best when free, but on this broad continent not a single man of your race is made the equal of a single man of ours. Go where you are treated the best, [New Granada]. . . . It is better for us both, therefore, to be separated." In "An Address on Colonization to a Negro Deputation at Washington (14 August 1862)," in *The Life and Writings of Abraham Lincoln*, 715-16.

[32]Noll, "The Image of the U.S. as a Biblical Nation, 1776–1865," 40.

[33]"Proclamation for a National Fast Day (March 30, 1863)," in *The Life and*

Lincoln viewed the Civil War as a test of America's greatness, prosperity, and destiny—and as a judgment from God.[34] The continuation of the hatred and bloodshed displayed throughout the war had to stop. For Lincoln, slavery and secession did not necessarily cause the war. Instead, an entire nation that had turned away from God was the cause. For Lincoln, a return to a unified America demanded a return to biblical values, and he attempted to (re)construct America out of the stories and sayings of the Bible.

American Unity—Myth or Reality?

Lincoln attempted to use biblical language to create and construct an American myth in which difference and conflict between white partisans were easily forgiven and forgotten, in which a nationwide sense of love and unity—among whites—could be reinstated. Yet Lincoln's American myth did not address the problem of what a true American is. For Lincoln, it seemed his myth was based upon the Union victory that at the time seemed assured and imminent.

Lincoln viewed America and the American myth from the standpoint of Union hegemony and victory. For Lincoln, his American myth of unity always assumed the hegemony of the North. Even today, more than one hundred years after the Civil War, the South is often viewed as a culturally inferior region, which must "catch up" to the rest of America.

While Lincoln's legacy was the construction of an American myth based upon reconciliation, including the removal of difference, such reconciliation was far from the reality. The South, while unified in name with the North, and rhetorically unified under one God, had often considered itself a region with its own identity. While the South became more "American" at the end of the Civil War, it simultaneously became more Southern. According to Robert Penn Warren, "The War claimed the Confederate states for

---

Writings of Abraham Lincoln, 752.
[34]"Second Inaugural Address," 842.

the Union, but at the same time, paradoxically, it made them more Southern. . . . In defeat, the Solid South was born."[35]

Did North and South, slave and slaveholder, white, Black, and Indian, get along better after Lincoln's proclamation for unity? Almost certainly not. But that was not important. What was important was that Americans *imagined* themselves to be more loving, less malicious, more nationalistic, and more American. With the help of Lincoln, Americans could once again hope for unity in the face of violence, death, and, in the case of the South, defeat, even if that unity never materialized.

The Rhetoric of Unity, Identity, and Hegemony

> The Wonderful World of Disney is more than a logo; it signifies how the terrain of popular culture has become central to com-modifying memory and rewriting narratives of national identity and global expansion. —Henry Giroux[36]

Why is *re*-writing, *re*-reading, and *re*-constructing such an important task? Not only for Walt Disney World, but for politicians, preachers and biblical scholars? I would argue that reconstruction is important because as communities undergo change, they are in desperate need to redefine themselves in the midst of that change. More specifically, cultural hegemony adapts in order to maintain its position.

Lincoln needed to redefine community in the midst of the Civil War, Walt Disney World continually adapts its stories and myths to the events surrounding America and the greater world, and preachers and biblical scholars attempt to relate the Bible to the changes in their worlds. But the rhetoric of unity is not deconstruction; it is redefinition, readaptation and modification vis-à-vis the same old myths.

In *American Mythologies*, Marshall Blonsky questions how it is that something comes to be read. Blonsky does not read books, he

---

[35]Robert Penn Warren, *The Legacy of the Civil War: Meditations on the Centennial* (New York: Random House, 1961) 14.

[36]Henry A. Giroux, *Disturbing Pleasures: Learning Popular Culture* (New York: Routledge, 1994) 31.

reads culture. His reading is simultaneously an exercise in how he reads and what he chooses to read. He "reads" fashion, "reads" culinary cuisine, "reads" pornography, and "reads" television.[37] For example, Blonsky realized that caviar's *function* is not only for nutritional consumption, but various kinds of consumption, uncovering the dynamics of meaning, or the dynamics of *meaning making* that seem to rule culture:

> What we discussed, I regret to say, was the *idea* of caviar, not caviar. There I was with a princess of gastronomy and what I imbibed was the *sign* of caviar, not caviar . . . for the function of caviar, about which we were speaking at table, is to salute one's guests, to include them in a tiny community of the unique where they can imagine themselves stars, celebrities, top of the heap, the very content of American desire.[38]

What should be understood is that in America, something like caviar is always propelled into the realm of sign, of idea, or of culture and imagination. Caviar is food, but Blonsky uncovers the greater meaning of caviar, defining precisely *who* the consumers of caviar *want* to be: "stars, celebrities, top of the heap, the very content of American desire." Lincoln's use of the Bible attempted to define a near-universal community much in the way caviar defined a seemingly small and elite community.

The same thing happened at Walt Disney World. I sat next to my cousin (a native of Korea) watching her with amusement as she attempted to identify the different countries represented in "It's a Small World." "India," she would say, or "France . . . Mexico." When she found two figures from Korea, a boy and a girl dressed in traditional Korean costume, she suddenly became more relaxed and happy. Now, she could include herself in Disney's myth. She belonged to the world according to Disney. Even though ninety-nine percent of the attractions at Walt Disney World did not have any depictions of Asians, it no longer mattered. She saw

---

[37]Marshall Blonsky, *American Mythologies* (New York: Oxford University Press, 1992).
[38]Ibid., 75.

"herself" once and that was enough. Obviously, she had not read Said's *Orientalism*.

In the same way, Lincoln's reading of the Bible revealed much about America and religion. His reading did not attempt to find an objective truth in the Bible—if there was or is such a thing. Instead, using the Bible, Lincoln created a world that attempted to construct a set of truths about America and Americans. He wanted Americans to see themselves in much same way as a consumer of caviar sees himself/herself as "a star," or as my cousin saw herself, as part of the Disney myth.

Finally, unity must not be confused with equality. In America, unity usually implies an inequality. A dominance of one group over another. Unity for Lincoln worked because the North was going to win. My cousin, as a foreigner to America, was grateful for a chance to see "herself" reflected in America, something she never imagined could happen. Unity is often used to cover up inequalities in society. As a reflection of American cultural, political, economic, and military dominance of the world, not unlike the position that the Roman empire enjoyed at a point in history, Disney could afford (unofficially on behalf of America) to make an appeal to world unity—American style.

Conclusion

The rhetoric of unity mythologizes something that can never exist—unity. The most to which this rhetoric can aspire is hegemony disguised as unity. The reason unity cannot work is because difference, diversity, and change represent fluidity and destabilization, while unity attempts to "freeze" some historical moment and interpret it as canonical. Some would say Lincoln succeeded in unifying the nation. But in light of the historical identity that they developed just after the Civil War and continued up to the recent past to cultiuvate, I would argue that Lincoln merely forced the South to temporarily succumb to the hegemony of the North.

Yet the power of this reheotrical strategy was not lost on politicians and other orators and institutions. Others continue to attempt goals similar to those Lincoln enunciated. Some of us feverishly hold on to these goals. We are mesmerized when we see ourselves in the mythic representations, joyful at our inclusion in the myth.

We are mesmerized when we see ourselves in the myths and stories of the public sphere, joyful at our "inclusion" in the myth. Not only in "It's a Small World," a presidential speech, or a preacher's sermon, but in a sneaker commercial, a movie, or the Olympics.

This is the good and bad news of rhetoric, reconstruction, and myth. They work. And they don't. They work in the sense that the appearance of unity is there, the feeling of inclusion can be quite real, and the world does hold together somehow. Just mention the two words, "Abraham Lincoln" to a politician in Washington D.C. and watch him or her speak of integrity, peace, and harmony. Or just watch the gleeful squeal of children when you tell them that you are going to see the next Disney movie. That is real.

On the other hand, apart from carefully constructed and more realistic and complicated situations, one may find that the myth has disappeared, only to be consumed, like a spoonful of caviar, at a later time more easily manipulated.

Charles Augustus Briggs, Modernism, and the Rise of Biblical Scholarship in Nineteenth-Century America

Doug Hill

Some historical figures are interesting because they are ahead of their time, others because they seem to embody their time. Charles Augustus Briggs (1841–1913) was of the latter variety.

On account of his championing the use of historical criticism of the Bible, which he was convinced would bring Christianity into the modern age, Briggs became one of the more notorious figures of late-nineteenth-century American Protestantism. "Higher criticism" had been winning converts and creating debate in America since the beginning of the nineteenth century. But its impact had been limited mostly to the academy—until 20 January 1891.[1] On that evening, Briggs gave his inaugural speech as the first occupant of the Edward Robinson Chair of Biblical Studies at Union Theological Seminary in New York.[2] The title of his address was "The

---

[1]Jerry Wayne Brown, *The Rise of Biblical Criticism in America, 1800–1870: The New England Scholars* (Middletown CT: Wesleyan, 1969) 180. Brown writes: "The strangest feature of American critical biblical studies in this early period is the fact that they vanished so quickly and made so little impact on the development of American religion after the Civil War. When Charles Briggs accepted appointment to the Edward Robinson Professorship at Union Theological Seminary in 1890 and pronounced his agreement on certain points of German higher criticism, it was generally thought that something new had been introduced to America."

[2]The position was named after Edward Robinson, one of Union seminary's earliest and most famous professors, and one of America's early advocates of historical criticism. See Brown, *The Rise of Biblical Criticism in America*, chap. 7; and Mark S. Massa, *Charles Augustus Briggs and the Crisis of Historical Criticism*, HDR 25 (Minneapolis: Fortress Press, 1990) 30-31, 84.

Authority of Holy Scripture," and it became one of the most controversial speeches in American church history. Among its results were two heresy trials, a media extravaganza, and the disengagement of Union Theological Seminary from the Presbyterian denomination.

"Dr. Briggs in his study at home." By courtesy of the Burke Library
of Union Theological Seminary in the City of New York.

Why did "The Authority of Holy Scripture" have the impact it did? Timing had a lot to do with it. The speech came at a critical juncture in American history, a point of confluence at which a host of social, cultural, and ecclesiastical trends converged. These trends had been building for years, and they involved historical shifts of major proportions. Charles Briggs—a man with a great talent for creating trouble, sometimes intentionally, sometimes not—provided the catalytic spark that ignited a vast store of accumulated energy with explosive force.

The central thesis of Briggs's address was that there are three sources of divine authority: the church, human reason, and the Bible.[3] Different people could find any one of these sources most amenable to their own pursuit of faith. A Catholic might lean more heavily on the church than on scripture. A rationalist would be naturally inclined to seek divinity through the avenues of the mind. Protestants, Briggs believed, tended to build their faith on scripture, while too often deprecating church and reason as legitimate means to the same end.[4] Worse, he said, was the fact that various "barriers" had been erected over the centuries that blocked these routes to God, especially to the Bible. He enumerated six obstacles to biblical faith, including the doctrines of inerrancy and verbal inspiration, an overreliance on miracles and prophecy, and the tendency to turn the Bible into a magical object.[5]

Although these themes contained plenty of fuel for controversy, the uproar that greeted Briggs's speech had as much to do with the belligerence of his rhetoric as it did with his arguments. His denunciation of "Bibliotary" was a typical example of the overall tone. Briggs declared that

> The Bible has no magical virtue in it, and there is no halo enclosing it. It will not stop a bullet any better than a mass-book. It will not keep off evil spirits any better than a cross. It will not guard a home from fire half so well as holy water. . . . The bible, as a book, is paper, print, and binding,—nothing more.[6]

---

[3]Charles Augustus Briggs, *The Authority of Holy Scripture: An Inaugural Address* (New York: Charles Scribner's Sons, 1891). (Subsequent editions of Briggs's inaugural address [³1891; ⁴1893; etc.] included a preface and an appendix containing additional notes and explanations, the charges of heresy, and Briggs's response to the charges of heresy before the presbytery of New York.)

[4]Ibid., 25-27.

[5]Ibid., 29-38.

[6]Ibid., 30.

Briggs showed no greater delicacy in discussing historical doubts about the authorship of the Bible.

> Traditionalists are crying out that [historical criticism] is destroying the Bible, because it is exposing their fallacies and follies. It may be regarded as the certain result of the science of the Higher Criticism that Moses did not write the Pentateuch or Job; Ezra did not write the Chronicles, Ezra, or Nehemiah; Jeremiah did not write the Kings or Lamentations; David did not write the Psalter, but only a few of the Psalms; Solomon did not write the Song of Songs or Ecclesiastes, and only a portion of the Proverbs; Isaiah did not write half of the book that bears his name. The great mass of the Old Testament was written by authors whose names or connection with their writings are lost in oblivion.[7]

Throughout the speech Briggs kept returning to the "traditionalists" who refused to accept the truths of historical criticism, condemning them to the dustbin of history with a contempt that was not even thinly veiled.

> We have undermined the breastworks of traditionalism, let us blow them to atoms. We have forced our way through the obstructions; let us remove them from the face of the earth. . . . For the dogmatism of mere traditional opinion and of the dogmaticians, I have no respect.[8]

The ferocity of this attack was widely noted at the time, and not only by Briggs's enemies. One of his Union colleagues, noted church historian Philip Schaff, wrote in a review of the case a year after the controversy exploded that Briggs had stated his views in such a "defiant and exasperating tone" that the address

> sounded like a manifesto of war and aroused at once a most determined opposition on the part of the conservative and orthodox press. Even some of his best friends deemed it unwise and uncalled for. [It was this] aggressive style and manner which brought on the fight. The inaugural created a sort of panic, as if

---

[7]Ibid., 37
[8]Ibid., 41, 63.

the Bible were in danger and the way opened for the teaching of downright rationalism in a leading institution of the Presbyterian Church."[9]

The Modernist Assault

As is clear from reading the voluminous newspaper coverage that the Briggs affair received, Schaff's use of the word "panic" was exactly right in conveying the reaction to Briggs's inaugural address, and in indicating the degree to which Briggs set larger cultural forces in motion than he probably expected.[10] What Schaff failed to acknowledge was that, although Briggs may not have consciously intended to provoke the response that ensued, his rhetoric accurately reflected his feelings. The inaugural address *was* a declaration of war—modernism against traditionalism.[11]

By modernism I mean the wide array of social, cultural, and psychological changes that accompanied the increasing dominance of nineteenth-century American culture by science, technology, and industrialism. There was a feeling when Briggs delivered his speech that all bets were off, that America was rushing pell-mell into the future, and that nothing would ever be the same. Some Americans, Briggs among them, anticipated those changes with

---

[9]Quoted in Richard L. Christensen, *The Ecumenical Orthodoxy of Charles Augustus Briggs* (Lewiston NY: Edwin Mellen Press, 1995) 97. Note that although Schaff was best known as a professor of church history, he taught at a time when departmental boundaries were far less distinctly defined than they are today, and during his long tenure at Union he held many posts, including professor of sacred literature, Hebrew, and apologetics. The same applied to other Union professors in Briggs's era. See Robert T. Handy, *A History of Union Theological Seminary in New York* (New York: Columbia University Press, 1987) 50-51 and passim.

[10]Union's Seminary's president at the time, Thomas Hastings, collected twelve volumes of newspaper clippings on the Briggs controversy and trials. These clippings are part of the Charles A. Briggs Collection at Union's Burke Library in New York City.

[11]Many modernists of the era besides Briggs used combative rhetoric in their attacks on traditionalism. A characteristic example was the title of Andrew Dickson White's opus, *A History of the Warfare of Science with Theology in Christendom* (New York: D. Appleton, 1898). Paul A. Carter comments on this and gives other examples in *The Spiritual Crisis of the Gilded Age* (DeKalb IL: Northern Illinois University Press, 1971) 18-19, 220.

boundless confidence and enthusiasm. Others were more cautious; some were plainly disturbed.[12] In the opening of his address, Briggs homed in with a sort of brutish instinct on the hunger for certainty and authority that had developed in response to that ever-accelerating drumbeat of change. He said:

> If we undertake to search the forms of authority that exist about us, they all alike disclose themselves as human and imperfect, and we feel at times as if we were on an unknown sea, with pilots and officers in whom we have no confidence. The earnest spirit presses back of all these human authorities in quest of an infallible guide and of an eternal and immutable certainty. Probability might be the guide of life in the superficial eighteenth century, and for those who have inherited its traditions, but the men of the present times are in quest of certainty.[13]

Briggs's mission was to answer that "quest of certainty" by presenting a new Christian apology that would make faith in God and Jesus credible in the modern world. Darwinism, the competing claims of other world religions—to which Western readers had only recently been exposed—new translations of the Bible, and the findings of biblical criticism all presented fundamental challenges to religious assumptions that had prevailed for centuries.[14] In order to accommodate these new facts of spiritual and intellectual life, Briggs constructed a theology in which change was seen as a virtue, rather than a threat. Drawing on the teachings of such German thinkers as Freidrich A. G. Tholuck, Isaac Dorner, and Emil Roediger (themselves influenced by Hegel, Schleiermacher,

---

[12]For background on the period, see Carter, *Spiritual Crisis*; Martin Marty, *Modern American Religion*, vol. 1, *The Irony of It All, 1893–1919* (Chicago: University of Chicago Press, 1986); and Arthur M. Schlesinger, Sr., *A Critical Period in American Religion, 1875–1900* (Philadelphia: Fortress Press, 1967). (Schlesinger was first published in *Massachusetts Historical Society Proceedings* 64 [October 1930–June 1932]: 523-46.)

[13]Briggs, *Inaugural Address*, 23-24.

[14]See Carter, *Spiritual Crisis*; Schlesinger, *A Critical Period*, passim. For discussion of the impact of the introduction of the Revised Version of the Bible (the revised New Testament was published in 1881; the Old Testament in 1885; the Apocrypha in 1889), see Peter J. Thusen, "Some Scripture Is Inspired by God: Late-Nineteenth-Century Protestants and the Demise of the Common Bible," *Church History* 65/4 (December 1996): 609-23.

and others), as well as the philosophy of his mentor at Union Seminary, Henry Boynton Smith, Briggs argued that God's revelation was continual and progressive through history.[15] The Bible was a chronicle of that revelation, but its underlying truths needed to be excavated from the words and thoughts of the various human sources through whom God's pure inspiration had been channeled. This excavation was a task that required both rigorous scholarship, using the tools of historical criticism, and the guidance of the Holy Spirit. In a letter to Henry Boynton Smith, written in 1867 while Briggs was still a student in Berlin, Briggs expressed the characteristic view of this school that the Lord was immanent through all creation, including the Bible:

> Now there is an unmistakable difference in the theological statements of the various authors of the O.T., which a general reading will disclose; but these differences will—I am confident— when properly studied, show a true and higher harmony—a unity all the more striking from the diversity of the elements.[16]

A corollary of this "biblical theology" (as Briggs termed his hermeneutic approach) was that traditional views of the Bible worked against the discovery of that underlying unity by freezing interpretation in place; the truth of one point in history was claimed to be the single true interpretation for all time. For Briggs, this was tantamount to blocking the ongoing guidance of the Holy Spirit, a position he defined as false orthodoxy. "That man or church whose orthodoxy does not make progress, ceases thereby to be orthodox, and from the necessities of the case becomes heterodox," Briggs wrote in his 1889 manifesto, *Whither?*

> He refuses to accept the truth that is offered him by the advances in science, philosophy, history, and more exact study of the

---

[15]Both Massa, *Charles Augustus Briggs and the Crisis of Historical Criticism*, and Christensen, *The Ecumenical Orthodoxy of Charles Augustus Briggs*, provide excellent discussions of Briggs's theology, its formation, and its sources. See 30-43 in Massa and 7-19 in Christensen.

[16]Quoted in Christensen, *The Ecumenical Orthodoxy of Charles Augustus Briggs*, 18.

sacred Scriptures. He is heterodox, in that he falls short of the revealed truth that the truly orthodox have already accepted.[17]

This self-consciously progressive view pitted Briggs against the traditional wisdom of the Presbyterian denomination in general and the orthodox divines at Princeton Theological Seminary in particular. A. A. Hodge, Benjamin Warfield, William Henry Green, and others held fast to the tenets of Scottish Common Sense Realism, which evangelicals since the early nineteenth century had hailed as "the royal road to truth."[18] The central hermeneutic claim of the Common Sense school was that biblical truth and scientific truth were in perfect harmony.[19] The Bible could be studied, just as nature could be studied, and it would reveal, objectively, God's revelation to humankind. The essence of this view was that truth was unchanging and eternal: God had poured out "His" Word in the Bible, once and for all. In its original autographs, therefore, the Bible was inerrant. Apparent errors, falsehoods, or inconsistencies were just that: apparent, nothing more than the illusions of critics who thought they knew better than the Lord. William Henry Green typified the Princetonian view when he analyzed the critics' deconstructions of the Pentateuch and came away unimpressed:

> May we not say of the latest critical attempt to roll the Penta-
> teuch off its old foundation, that it has not achieved success? It
> has enveloped Mt. Blanc in a cloud of mist, and proclaimed that

---

[17]Charles Briggs, *Whither? A Theological Question for the Times*, 3rd ed. (New York: Charles Scribner's Sons, 1890; [1]1889) 8-9.

[18]Mark A. Noll, *Between Faith and Criticism: Evangelicals, Scholarship, and the Bible in America* (San Francisco: Harper & Row, 1986) 15. For discussions of the influence of the Common Sense school on American Protestantism, see Theodore Dwight Bozeman, *Protestants in an Age of Science: The Baconian Ideal and Antebellum American Religious Thought* (Chapel Hill NC: University of North Carolina Press, 1977). For a shorter but lucid discussion of the central issues, see George M. Marsden, "Everyone One's Own Interpreter? The Bible, Science, and Authority in Mid-Nineteenth-Century America," in *The Bible in America: Essays in Cultural History*, ed. Nathan O. Hatch and Mark A. Noll (New York: Oxford University Press, 1982) 79-95. For a still briefer discussion, see Marty, *Modern American Religion*, 232-36.

[19]Marsden, "Everyone One's Own Interpreter?" 86.

its giant cliffs had forever disappeared. But, lo, the mist blows away, and the everlasting hills are still in place.[20]

Clearly, the respective convictions of Briggs and the Princetonians regarding the nature of biblical revelation put them on a collision course, and collide they did, first in the pages of their jointly published journal, *Presbyterian Review*, and ultimately in the ecclesiastical courts.[21] There was irony in the fact that the Princetonian position was advanced as if it represented the unquestioned wisdom of the ages when in reality it simply represented an earlier accommodation to the same challenge from Enlightenment rationalism Briggs was trying to face. Both positions claimed to be scientific, and both were based on an assumption that an objective truth could be found. The conviction that truth was attainable, and that the application of inductive reasoning and democracy would attain it, was one of the prevailing American mythologies of the late nineteenth century. Given enough freedom and enough facts, the thinking went, the truth would always emerge. "Imperfect statements will be corrected by progress," Briggs said in his inaugural address. "All forms of error will disappear before the breath of truth."[22]

Observers of this period have pointed out that neither the liberals nor the conservatives in the debate over historical criticism were as scientific as they claimed to be.[23] Both camps accepted without question, for example, that Jesus Christ was the Son of

---

[20]Quoted in Noll, *Between Faith and Criticism*, 22.

[21]Some of Briggs's opponents from Princeton, especially William Henry Green, played leading roles in his prosecution on heresy charges. For background on the *Presbyterian Review*, see Massa, *Charles Augustus Briggs*, 53-54. Also see Mark A. Noll, ed., *The Princeton Defense of Plenary Verbal Inspiration* (New York: Garland, 1988); and Doug Hill, "Defending the Faith at Princeton" (unpublished paper, Union Theological Seminary, Spring 1997).

[22]Briggs, "Authority of Holy Scripture," 63. Also see Marsden, "Everyone One's Own Interpreter?" 83, 90; and Carter, *Spiritual Crisis*, 33. The association of democratic freedom with the pursuit of scientific truth is a central theme of Marsden's *The Soul of the American University: From Protestant Establishment to Established Nonbelief* (New York: Oxford University Press, 1994). See, e.g., 85, 109, and esp. his discussions of John Dewey, 174-75, 251, 298, 306.

[23]See Marty, *Modern American Religion*, 26; and James P. Wind, *The Bible and the University: The Messianic Vision of William Rainey Harper* (Atlanta GA: Scholars Press, 1987) 63.

God and that he had been resurrected from the dead. Their theologies reflected a desire to answer the rationalist challenge by using terminology that *sounded* scientific, thereby assuming, they hoped, an aura of scientific certainty by association. The contradictions in their positions were noted by skeptics of the time and promptly exploited, substantially weakening their credibility with both believers and skeptics.[24] The notorious atheist, Col. Robert Ingersoll, for example, described Charles Briggs's views as containing "too much science for a churchman and too much superstition for a scientist," a split that left him, Ingersoll said, "with his feet in the gutter and his head in the clouds."[25]

Understanding why Christian apologists of the nineteenth century went through such contortions is easier if one appreciates how vulnerable they felt the state of American Protestant piety to have been. Briggs, writing in a more moderate tone than was his custom, described religion's "very unsatisfactory condition" in the opening paragraph of *Whither?*

> There is a widespread dissatisfaction with the Old Theology, and the old methods of worship and church work. At the same time there is distrust and anxiety with reference to new theology and new measures that are proposed by recent theological doctors. The ministers are not preaching the distinctive doctrines of the Old Theology, or the peculiar features of their denominations, because the people are tired of them, and will not have them. The ministers do not care to preach to empty pews, and besides, not a few of the ministers sympathize with their people in these matters. The ministers are in feverish condition. Some are desirous of adapting the Old Theology and old methods to the new conditions and circumstances; others are opposed to any changes in the old types; there are some hot champions of the new, and

---

[24]See Marsden, *The Soul of the American University*, 93; and Carter, *Spiritual Crisis*, 35-36.

[25]Robert G. Ingersoll, "Professor Briggs," in *The Works of Robert G. Ingersoll in Twelve Volumes*, vol. 12, ed. C. P. Farrell (New York: C. P. Farrell: Ingersoll Publishers, 1900) 312. There was an irony in this comment of which Ingersoll may not have been aware, given that Briggs was an adherent of the "mediating philosophy" endorsed by Isaac Dorner and Henry B. Smith, a philosophy which quite consciously tried to walk a middle line between rationalism and orthodoxy. See Massa, *Charles Augustus Briggs*, 31.

there are some sturdy defenders of the old; but the majority do not care to disturb the peace, and are waiting for light and guidance.[26]

Objective evidence that there was in fact widespread religious malaise during this period is inconclusive.[27] On the one hand, church membership appeared to be rising,[28] revivalists like Dwight L. Moody seemed to be thriving,[29] and polls showed that college students were attending church services in substantial numbers.[30] On the other hand, other polls showed widespread agnosticism and doubt on campus;[31] the letters and diaries of thousands of average citizens revealed them agonizing over losses of faith;[32] contemporary newspaper accounts frequently discussed a growing irreligiosity;[33] and the success of such skeptics as Ingersoll, Felix Adler (founder of the Ethical Cultural Society), the evolutionist Henry Drummond, Cornell University President Andrew Dickson White, and *Monist* editor Paul Carus showed that religious doubt was not only an acceptable topic in public forums, but a popular one.[34] "Whether or not there was a general withering of faith, many articulate observers evidently thought there was," writes historian Paul A. Carter in *The Spiritual Crisis of the Gilded Age*.[35] Carter quotes an article in *The Forum* in 1896 which stated flatly that "Christianity appears to many of the wisest to be at the present day in deadlier peril than it has been at any time during the eighteen hundred years of its existence."[36] Briggs himself, in a

---

[26]Briggs, *Whither?*, 1.

[27]Paul A. Carter discusses this question at length in *The Spiritual Crisis of the Gilded Age*. See preface and chap. 1.

[28]Martin Marty has concluded there was a genuine rise despite notoriously unreliable membership data. See *Modern American Religion*, 153-54.

[29]Carter, *Spiritual Crisis*, viii-ix.

[30]Marsden, *The Soul of the American University*, 176.

[31]Ibid., 163.

[32]Marty, *Modern American Religion*, 35.

[33]There is ample evidence of this concern in the twelve volumes of newspaper coverage of the Briggs trials collected by Union President Thomas Hastings.

[34]These names appear frequently both in the contemporary literature of the period and in histories. See, e.g., Schlesinger, *A Critical Period in American Religion*, 11.

[35]Carter, *Spiritual Crisis*, 10.

[36]Ibid.

Forum article entitled "The Alienation of Church and People," declared, "We are living in the ebb-time of the Christian Church."[37]

It was this perceived crisis of faith that caused Briggs so passionately to proclaim historical criticism as the means by which scripture and modern science could be reconciled. One can almost sense his anguish when he said in his inaugural address that "the best men of our age" no longer take the Bible seriously, and that they view traditional claims of biblical authority with "disgust."[38] Although not quite as rhetorically aggressive, the traditionalists were equally disdainful of what they saw as pitiful and dangerous attempts to undermine the wisdom of the ages with the dangerous distractions of the moment. One of Briggs's most implacable foes was William G. T. Shedd, the only Union professor to side publicly against him.[39] Shedd wrote in a newspaper essay the month after Briggs's inaugural address that his first objection to historical criticism was that it was "wholly modern":

> This to many persons, would be a recommendation. But in estimating theories, if time is to be taken into account, one that has all time behind it is preferable to one that has only a fraction. To be modern is a good recommendation for the fashion of a hat, but not for an opinion in science."[40]

Being identified with either the "modern" or the "traditional" camp in the Briggs affair often seemed to have as much to do with the self-identity associated with those labels as it did with the specific theological positions they ostensibly defined. Where one stood in relation to the tumultuous changes of the age was obviously a matter of tremendous psychological importance.[41] Predict-

---

[37]Charles Briggs, "The Alienation of Church and People," *The Forum* 16/3 (November 1893): 366.

[38]Briggs, *Inaugural Address*, 33, 40.

[39]Shedd had replaced Edward Robinson on the Union faculty when Robinson died. See Handy, *Union Theological Seminary*, 39.

[40]*New York Independent*, 19 February 1891. Note that all newspaper clippings quoted in this paper are from the scrapbooks on the Briggs trials collected by Thomas Hastings. Many articles in this collection are undated; many do not include the name of the publication in which they appeared; very few show page numbers.

[41]Marshall Blonsky has written cogently, and humorously, of the vital impor-

ably, students were among Charles Briggs's staunchest, and loudest, supporters; the outrage over his inaugural address was exacerbated by the fact that the students in the audience applauded loudest for the sections that were most provocative.[42]

Newspapers, too, seemed anxious to use the Briggs controversy as an opportunity to promote themselves as either boldly modern or solidly traditional. The *New York Times* was perhaps the most vocal in its support of biblical criticism. When Briggs won his second acquittal on heresy charges, the *Times* headline called it "A triumph for progressive thought in the church" and dismissed conservatives who objected to the verdict as "soreheads."[43] In an earlier editorial, Briggs was said to be guilty only of

> bringing the Presbyterian church into harmony with the advanced and intelligent [interpretation] of the Bible which is the chief modern mark of religious progress. The persons who are forcing this issue may be friends or enemies to Dr. Briggs, but they are automatons in the grasp of stronger forces than they acknowledge. . . . The religious strength is with the conservatives, but the lead of the future is with the liberals, and whatever may be done with Prof. Briggs as an individual, the great working forces of the time are with him. . . . [T]he movement which he is urging forward is a movement common to intelligent minds everywhere. The Protestant theory of the inerrancy of the Bible has been given up by these men and the present methods used in its interpretation are bringing out its study as a whole and giving us a more complete knowledge of what it teaches than has before been obtained. Dr. Briggs is simply a fellow worker with other scholars in the common enterprise of formulating a new biblical theology, and no action of the Presbyterian church will be more than a temporary interruption of his purpose.[44]

---

tance of identity in the modern era. See *American Mythologies* (New York: Oxford University Press, 1992). Wesley A. Kort addressed this same point in *"Take Read": Scripture, Textuality, and Cultural Practice* (University Park PA: Pennsylvania State University Press, 1996) 10. Beliefs in our culture often change, he wrote, "because of the lingering notion that to have them is to be unenlightened and that full enfranchisement in the culture is tied to dissolving them."

[42]*New York Sun*, 12 February 1891.
[43]*New York Times*, 1 January 1893.
[44]*New York Times*, 17 May 1891.

The Impunity of Expertise

The identification of Briggs as a "scholar" was a label that in the late nineteenth century carried an especially powerful connotation. This was the dawning of the age of the expert, a major shift in American intellectual and cultural life, and biblical criticism was in the vanguard of that movement.[45] Like most of his colleagues on the Union faculty, Briggs had studied historical criticism in Germany,[46] so he was among those who helped import to the United States Germanic intellectual ideas and orientation to scholarship. According to historian Jungen Herbst, prior to the nineteenth century, higher education in the United States typically constituted a broad, generalized curriculum based mainly on the classics, usually capped in the final year with a foundational course on moral philosophy. Professors were generalists, usually clergymen who taught the full range of courses. The German model, by contrast, emphasized specialized training in a single field. Extensive research within that specialty was required, and it was up to the individual scholar to decide what course of study best served his or her individual academic needs. The motivating ideal, Herbst says, was an unobstructed search for truth, a philosophy that held obvious appeal for Americans, particularly young Americans frustrated by the strictures of traditionalism.[47]

Like many young Christians from the United States, Briggs had problems with the lack of reverence he found in German academic circles, but in a revealing letter to Henry Boynton Smith, he made it clear he also had little use for reverence without scholarship.

> In exegesis there is a very great want in America. Here every great theologian is an Exegete. They are too much influenced by rationalism as we would say in America, and this is perhaps

---

[45]See Jungen Herbst, *The German Historical School in American Scholarship* (Ithaca NY: Cornell University Press, 1965) chaps. 1–4. James Wind's *The Bible and the University*, Mark Noll's *Between Faith and Criticism*, and George Marsden's *The Soul of the American University* also examine this shift at length.

[46]See Handy, *Union Theological Seminary*, chaps. 2–4.

[47]Herbst, *German Historical School*, 30-31.

because they have thought more deeply and candidly upon the subjects and seen the difficulties and tired to grapple with them. Whereas we have overlooked them or passed them by without examination; but in spite of their *coldness* in handling Scripture, it is more *satisfactory* to the student than a devotional spirit without *thought*.[48]

Given that affinity for disciplined, reasoned study, it made sense that criticism (both higher and lower) became fundamental to Briggs's theological views, a position that inevitably privileged the professional scholar over the amateur believer. "Criticism requires for its exercise careful training," he wrote in the 1890 edition of *Biblical Study*, his overview of critical methods.

Only those who have learned how to use its tools and have employed them with the best masters, and have attained a mastery of the departments of knowledge to be criticized, are prepared for the delicate and difficult work of criticism.[49]

This academic approach to spirituality was characteristic of the mainstream Presbyterianism of the day, but it was profoundly out-of-step with the revivalism that was moving much of the rest of the country, particularly the less-educated population.[50] Interestingly, Briggs himself had had a conversion experience at a revival meeting during his college days in South Carolina, and he considered his theology a mixture of intellectual and experiential piety.[51] But the evidence of his student letter to Henry Boynton Smith and the body of a lifetime of his writings shows that his true inclination was definitely toward the former.[52]

---

[48]Quoted in Christensen, *The Ecumenical Orthodoxy of Charles Augustus Briggs*, 14. For earlier American scholars who struggled with German impiety, see Brown, *The Rise of Biblical Criticism in America*, passim.

[49]Charles Augustus Briggs, *Biblical Study: Its Principles, Methods, and History* (New York: Charles Scribner's Sons, 1890) 80.

[50]See H. Richard Niebuhr, *The Social Sources of Denominationalism* (repr.: New York: Meridian, 1957; [1929]) 161.

[51]Massa, *Charles Augustus Briggs*, 27.

[52]James Wind has noted that in their mature professional lives both Briggs and William Rainey Harper seemed to downplay the conversion experiences of their youths. See *The Bible and the University*, 36-37.

Briggs was also sympathetic to the ongoing professionalization of American education as a whole. He was instrumental in the founding of one of the country's earliest academic professional associations, the Society of Biblical Literature and Exegesis, in 1880. Later in his career he led a campaign (against the resistance of most of his colleagues on the faculty) to add graduate courses at Union Seminary; eventually he hoped the school would evolve into a broad-based theological university.[53] More to the point, when the board of directors of Union Seminary was confronted with a choice between maintaining its affiliation with the Presbyterian denomination or supporting Briggs's right to pursue the scholarly path of his choice, it quickly chose the latter, marking a milestone in the ascendancy of academic autonomy over denominational control in American higher education.[54]

Briggs's identity as a scholar played a significant role throughout his trials. "They say," wrote the *New York Sun*, "that Prof. Briggs is so erudite, has delved so deeply into the origin of Christianity and its systems that there are many ministers who, holding fast to the faith, yet fear to attack him lest they be ignobly routed."[55] Briggs and his allies were openly contemptuous of those who opposed them, a contempt that presaged academic ostracism of fundamentalist believers for the next hundred years. When the Presbyterian General Assembly first voted that Briggs must be tried on charges of heresy, C. H. Parkhurst, a member of Union's board of directors, complained in a letter to the *New York Evangelist* that the theological issues involved had obviously been too complicated for the assembly to comprehend. "I doubt if one in twenty of the commissioners at Detroit would have dared to stand up in the presence of that company and attempt to state what the

---

[53]Briggs's initiative eventually failed. See Handy, *Union Theological Seminary*, 54, 108-10. For a largely negative assessment of the long-term impact of academic specialization on American seminary education, see Edward Farley, "Why Seminaries Don't Change: A Reflection on Faculty Specialization," *The Christian Century* (5-12 February 1997): 133-43.

[54]Massa, *Charles Augustus Briggs*, 104. In *The Soul of the American University*, George Marsden argues that in the long run this newfound "freedom" of religion in American universities turned out to be a decidedly mixed blessing for American Christianity.

[55]*New York Sun*, 12 April 1891.

higher criticism *is*," he wrote. "Their one impression seemed to be that it was a frightful doctrinal disease of some kind, and that Doctor Briggs had it in its most malignant form."[56]

At several crucial points in the controversy, noted theologians stepped forward in defense of Briggs. The *New York Herald* ran a long analysis by Philip Schaff, whose "international fame," the paper said, compelled respect from clergymen of all churches. Schaff concluded his essay with a rare burst of invective, writing that a conviction of Briggs would "drive all liberal and conscientious men into other churches and leave the Presbyterian seminaries empty or in the charge of old fogies who close their eyes against the truth."[57] The *New York World* ran a lengthy front-page article in which several of Briggs's peers at major universities around the country, including William Rainey Harper, president of the newly opened University of Chicago, and George P. Stevens, professor of New Testament History at Yale, were interviewed. All were staunch advocates of historical criticism; informed scholarship, they said, simply offered no alternative. This article bore the headline "Briggs's champions; Extraordinary utterances about the Bible; Errors and discrepancy; Learned theologians in the fight against dogmatism; Voices from the universities."[58]

With this sort of coverage Briggs's opponents were hard-pressed to counter the impression that the weight of modern scholarship was against them, so much so that in his second heresy trial they brought forth an expert of their own, Bible scholar J. J. Lampe, to present the prosecution's final argument. Lampe acknowledged that most people seemed to believe that Professor Briggs "knows more about the Bible than all his co-Presbyters taken together" and that the Presbyterians had taken a position in favor of a "narrow and superficial treatment of scripture." Nothing, Lampe argued, could be further from the truth. "There are many scholars as great as Dr. Briggs. And our church is in

---

[56]*New York Evangelist*, 11 June 1891.
[57]*New York Herald*, 17 May 1891.
[58]*New York World*, 31 May 1891.

hardy accord with the best scholarship. . . . It favors the best learning in every department of research and culture."[59]

It would not be long before the fundamentalists would essentially cede the battleground of scholarship to the liberals, a concession a few conservative intellectuals would struggle to reverse for much of the twentieth century.[60] In the meantime, it was clear to everyone in the Briggs case that what was at stake was not only biblical authority but doctrinal and ecclesiastical authority. A few weeks after Briggs delivered his inaugural address, the *New York Sun* wondered in an editorial why a lone renegade had been allowed to issue such pronouncements at all. The editorial suggested:

> As it is utterly subversive of all the standards of orthodoxy, the evangelical papers are asking whether the Presbyterian church as a whole ought not to deal with a subject so tremendously important. A revolution so complete, they think, should not be made by a single individual and a single institution on their own impulse only. . . . We do not see how it is possible for the General Assembly to avoid this question and escape the responsibility of deciding whether Briggs shall be allowed to continue as a professor of biblical theology in a Presbyterian divinity school.[61]

That Briggs would have the audacity to think he could redefine the meaning of scripture solely on the authority of his superior scholarship provoked enormous resentments; many Americans were not quite ready to defer to the experts solely on the experts' say-so, at least not on the subject of the Bible. When the New York Presbytery stymied the hopes of the General Assembly and acquitted Briggs in his second heresy trial, conservatives felt their church had been taken over.

> The regrettable thing about the verdict [reported the archconservative *Mail & Express*] is that it will appear to outsiders [as if the church is] accepting the scriptures as untrue upon the

---

[59]*New York Tribune,* 12 December 1892.

[60]See George M. Marsden, *Reforming Fundamentalism: Fuller Seminary and the New Evangelicalism* (Grand Rapids MI: Eerdmans, 1987).

[61]*New York Sun,* 12 February 1891.

authority of this erratic teacher. When the ministerial judges confront their congregations tomorrow morning, many of them may find that their people think they have pronounced, as agreeable to the Bible, and laws of their church, the assertions that the Bible is fallible, that reason can make a man a representative Christian as well as the scriptures, and that when our Lord taught a certain doctrine of the Old Testament, He taught what was not true.[62]

The editorial went on to express doubt "whether Christianity of that kind can speak with authority or success." Already, the *Mail & Express* reported, conversions in Presbyterian churches had declined, which was evidence, it said, of "the paralyzing effects of Briggsism." Now, with Briggs's acquittal, the editorial concluded, "the coolness may be expected to grow."[63]

That comment indicates the degree to which each side in the Briggs controversy blamed the other for the spread of skepticism in modern America. It also suggests how quickly the scholarly conclusions of historical criticism came to be associated in conservative minds with a lack of biblical faith, an association that would become another touchstone of the emerging fundamentalist movement.[64]

On Cities, Gentlemen, and Progress

As significant as the shift toward specialized expertise was in mainstream American culture, an even greater shift was also underway as the Briggs saga unfolded: the transition from a rural, agrarian society to a predominately urban, industrial one. In 1890, the U.S. Census Bureau declared that the Western settlement had progressed to the point that the American frontier should be considered officially closed, a turning point freighted with significance for the American psyche. (The census report was the jumping-off point for Frederick Jackson Turner's famous 1893 essay, "The Significance of the Frontier in American History.") Fears had been

---

[62]*Mail & Express*, 31 December 1892.
[63]Ibid.
[64]See Noll, *Between Faith and Criticism*; and Marsden, *Reforming Fundamentalism*, passim.

steadily building about the growing scarcity of affordable land, about the unchecked numbers of immigrants pouring into the country (many of them Catholic), about dirty, crime-ridden city streets, about the growing economic domination of land barons and monopoly capital, and about growing evidence of political corruption.[65] "The transformations through which the United States is passing in our own day," wrote Turner, "are so profound, so far-reaching, that it is hardly an exaggeration to say that we are witnessing the new birth of a new nation in America."[66]

All these fears challenged the treasured mythological view of America as the New Eden, a place of unbounded freedom and opportunity, unsullied by the corruption and restrictions of the Old World. There was a perception that the indomitable American spirit needed new frontiers to conquer. Such a perception fueled expansionist appetites for Cuba and the Philippines during this period.[67]

Even more pervasive was the conviction that a new and different American frontier was dawning in technology, science, industry, business, and education. Miraculous developments in all these areas, it was believed, were creating a new world order, one in which America would be the leader, not Europe. The idea that civilization was a massive locomotive moving steadily and triumphantly forward was trumpeted relentlessly during the late nineteenth century,[68] and Charles Briggs could not wait to get onboard—if only the traditionalists would let him.

---

[65]Frederick Jackson Turner, *The Frontier in American History* (Huntington NY: Robert E. Krieger, 1976). Also see David M. Wrobel, *The End of American Exceptionalism* (Lawrence KS: University Press of Kansas, 1993); and David W. Nobel, *The Progressive Mind, 1890–1917* (Chicago: Rand McNally, 1970).

[66]Martin Marty includes this quote in his discussion of the rise of the cities in *Modern American Religion* (see p. 55).

[67]See Nobel, *The Progressive Mind,* 20.

[68]Paul A. Carter discusses the worship of progress in late nineteenth-century America at length in *The Spiritual Crisis of the Gilded Age* (see chap. 8). Charles Mabee has described such beliefs as "the new American ideology," an ideology which he says is comprised of "an almost unlimited confidence" in technology combined with a flourishing "mythos of exceptionality and mission." See *Reading Sacred Texts Through American Eyes: Biblical Interpretation as Cultural Critique,* StABH 7 (Macon GA: Mercer University Press, 1991) 18-19.

There has never been a time [he wrote in *Whither?*] when the church had such a vast work to do for the Master. The possibilities for thinking and for working are wonderful—the ideals set before us are magnificent. All other departments of human learning are advancing, every other human enterprise is pushing with enormous energy. Is the Church of Jesus to drift along in the rear, too conservative to make any more progress than it is forced to make; too reactionary to be aggressive, except in attack upon those who would excite it by criticism and stimulate it by discoveries to take its proper place in the advancing host of God?[69]

For Briggs and his supporters, historical criticism became associated with the idea of progress almost as if it were a new invention, every bit as promising in its potential as the telephone or the electric lightbulb, thus, a vehicle of modernism that would help give birth to the new American century. Once again, it was the *New York Times* that best expressed the flavor of the progressive cause, comparing Briggs's acquittal in his first heresy trial to the conviction ten years earlier of William Robertson Smith on similar charges in Scotland. The Briggs verdict, the *Times* said in an editorial, proved that freedom of religious thought was one of the things that made the United States the leader in a world no longer hamstrung by outmoded ideas and customs.

To acquit him is to abandon the historic "standards." These are, in fact, abandoned as incredible by educated men of our generation, and the acquittal of Dr. Briggs amounts to an abandonment of them by the divines who voted for his acquittal. We may call this result "modern," but we have an equally good right to call it American.[70]

Briggs himself seemed to endorse the same position when he mentioned in *Biblical Study* that criticism needed to subject itself to constant scrutiny and review. He wrote that

---

[69]Briggs, *Whither?*, 267.
[70]*New York Times*, 17 May 1891.

Eternal vigilance is the price of truth as well as of liberty. Criticism improves its methods with the advancement of human learning. In the infancy or growth of a nation, or of an individual, or of the world, we do not find criticism. It belongs to the manhood and maturity of a nation and the world's civilization.[71]

This idealization of progress became entangled with two other important sources of tension in the Briggs case: class resentment, and the related tensions between urban and rural Americans. The massive shift in population during this period away from the farms and toward the cities helped implant in the American consciousness the oppositional stereotypes of the city slicker and country bumpkin, caricatures that expressed (and even continue to express) a deep ambivalence in the national psyche about the respective advantages and disadvantages—culturally, religiously, and otherwise—of both environments. The apotheosis of this dynamic, at least in terms of the way modern Americans view the Bible, was the Scopes trial of 1925; but the Briggs trials can be seen as opening acts of what became an epic conflict.

In the minds of many of Briggs's supporters, and in the minds of many of those who opposed him, Charles Briggs represented the quintessential New York gentleman of the Gilded Age. The son of the city's "barrel king,"[72] he was white, well off, and Presbyterian, which in the late nineteenth century was as close as an American was likely to get to royalty. "Surely," wrote one of Briggs's more socially conscious contemporaries, the Rev. Josiah Strong, "to be a Christian and an Anglo-Saxon and an American in this generation is to stand on the very mountaintop of privilege."[73] Union Theological Seminary itself was a self-consciously urban institution. From its beginnings the school's founders considered its city location to be a key element of its identity and purpose (its original name was New York Theological Seminary).

---

[71]Briggs, *Biblical Study*, 80.
[72]Massa, *Charles Augustus Briggs*, 26.
[73]Quoted in Marty, *Modern American Religion*, 24.

In order to shield students from the temptation of the city, no other seminary had been deliberately placed in the countryside.[74]

Newspaper coverage of the Briggs affair revealed how thoroughly the gentlemanly class dominated public affairs in New York at the time. It is fair to assume that the Briggs case was deemed newsworthy in the first place largely because the respectable press of the day defined Presbyterianism and respectability as virtually synonymous, and the twelve volumes of newspaper clippings on the case collected by Union President Thomas Hastings show that any issue of importance to the Presbyterians was deemed to have been newsworthy indeed.[75] Although the editorial bias of each paper for or against Briggs was usually clear, the coverage was more evenhanded than might be expected (perhaps, because there were prominent Presbyterians on both sides), and the tone was, with a few exceptions, deferential. Articles habitually gave the names and titles of every "gentleman" in attendance at a given hearing, speech or sermon—sometimes more than twenty names were listed—and the statements of prominent men were often run almost verbatim, many times occupying several columns of space.

Among the friendlier papers toward Briggs was the *New York World*, which profiled him as his first trial was about to begin.[76] The stacked headlines on the piece described him as "an early riser," a "frugal eater," and "a lover of music" whose three daughters assisted him "in his literary work." A pen and ink drawing showed Briggs reclining in a well-padded rocking chair, newspaper at hand, surrounded by books in his study (see p. 72, above). The article opened with the following description:

---

[74]Handy, *Union Theological Seminary*, 6-8.

[75]It should be noted that Hastings's scrapbooks represent an informal and by no means exhaustive collection of news articles concerning the Briggs case. Chronological gaps and inconsistencies are apparent. Hastings also may have exercised some editorial bias in choosing which articles to preserve, although the collection does include material which is unfavorable to Briggs.

[76]This clip is undated, but in the scrapbooks it is in proximity to articles on Briggs's first trial. Its content supports the assumption that the article would have appeared at that time.

> Dr. Charles Briggs, the alleged heretic, looked anything but the cold, common formal man his enemies would have the public believe as, yesterday morning, a little after eight o'clock, he tripped lightly down the broad oak stairway of his pleasant home, No. 120 West 93rd Street, and in an affable and courteous manner extended the greetings of the day to a representative of the *World*.
>
> Dr. Briggs is a man of slender form and has the calm, quiet ways of one who passes his days and nights in the endless world of books. He is considerably above the medium height. His hands are extremely small and white, and when he speaks it is in a low voice of peculiar charm and sweetness.[77]

The article went on to explain that Professor Briggs spent most of each weekday, from eight or so in the morning to midnight, working in his second-floor study, leaving only to deliver his lectures at Union Seminary. Callers were received in the parlor, and "messages of good will" were frequently dispatched to neighbors. For those who were ill or in need of counsel, the professor accorded "the charm of his personal presence."[78]

Amidst the voluminous attention paid to the gentlemen involved in the Briggs case, a glimmer of class consciousness occasionally slipped through. An example was the following gossip item from the *New York Sun*, which concerned the meetings of the Chi Alpha Club, an association of "prominent, mostly Presbyterian clergymen" in Manhattan.

> It is reported that at its meetings the plan of campaign of the Briggs party is discussed over fried oysters, vanilla ice cream, and sponge cake. It is said that at its meetings the young and tender pastors are initiated into the mysteries of the "new theology," and have a reason given them for the faith which is not in them. It is said to be at the Chi Alpha that impulsive brethren are instructed with regard to the errors of the Old Testament and learn to speak glibly of the mythology of Moses,

---

[77]Ibid.
[78]Ibid.

and they can discover how much Briggs has been misunderstood, and how not to be infidel is to be ignorant.[79]

This was an example of the sort of reverse snobbism that would later become a staple of tabloid journalism, but in Briggs's era such moments were rare, at least in the articles collected by President Hastings. Anyone outside the circle of men in power was mentioned only in passing, if at all. After one of the General Assembly votes against Briggs, for example, a reporter called at Hastings's home for comment, but "a servant" said he was out of the country.[80] Women ("the fair sex") were similarly invisible, being mentioned only as supportive family members or as auditors at Briggs's trials. A reporter covering one trial noted that the women in the gallery listened to the testimony so intently one would have thought they were preparing to cast their votes on its outcome.[81] This was meant as a joke. Another article carried a pen-and-ink drawing of a woman wearing a fancy hat sitting on a high-backed bench with her head bowed, dozing off. The caption read, "Too much theology."[82]

Although President Hastings's clippings are drawn overwhelmingly from New York papers, a few suggest the degree to which the hinterlands, then as now, viewed New York as standing at an uncomfortable distance from mainstream American values (despite what the *New York Times* might have believed). An editorial in a paper called the *Mid-Continent*, for example, conveyed a distinctly fundamentalist air when it accused Briggs of being more interested in self-aggrandizement than in Christian charity.

> If Briggs and kind were as zealous in the business of saving souls as they are monkeying for a fleeting notoriety, born of, and ministering to pride, they would understand God's word better, see straight, and aid the coming of that kingdom which is righteousness, peace, and joy in the holy Ghost. That is how the laity see it.[83]

---

[79]*New York Sun*, undated.
[80]Undated article.
[81]*New York Sun*, 5 November 1891.
[82]*New York Tribune*, 1 December 1892.
[83]Undated article.

When the New York Presbytery quickly dismissed the charges against Briggs in his first heresy trial, an editorial in the *New York Post* noted that the Presbyteries to the West had always considered the New York chapter "altogether too lax for the good of the denomination." Given that suspicion, the *Post* added a prediction: "In the present temper of the denomination at large, it is perfectly idle to say, as some make haste to say, that this is the end of the whole affair."[84]

The *Post's* editorialist was precisely on target. Consistently throughout the case, Briggs was acquitted by the members of the New York Presbytery only to have the acquittal reversed in the General Assembly, by huge margins. The penultimate motion in which the assembly voted to disregard Briggs's second acquittal, setting the stage for his expulsion from the ministry, went against him by a vote of 405 to 145.[85] The commissioners may not have been able to say what historical criticism was, exactly, but they apparently understood enough to know they did not like it.

Some Comments on the Limitations of Class

Paging through President Hastings's volumes of newspaper clippings on the Briggs case is a claustrophobic experience: it seems as if the entire affair took place in a closed, windowless room. The battle over historical criticism, and the parallel struggle over revision of the Westminster Confession, appear to have been all-consuming for those involved, while the world outside—a world filled with poverty, racism, political corruption and exploitation of labor, among other problems—did not seem to exist. True, during Briggs's ordeal there were frequent calls for peace, so that the church might get on with more pressing business, but there was no hint that that pressing business involved any great reform agenda left unpursued. Rather, the passions displayed in the heat of battle left the definite impression that for those involved, no issue on earth could have been more important than deciding the fate of Charles Augustus Briggs.

---

[84]*New York Post*, 5 November 1891.
[85]Massa, *Charles Augustus Briggs*, 106.

The insularity and elitism of the eastern Protestant establishment was widely recognized at the time. James McCosh, president of the College of New Jersey (later Princeton University) from 1868 to 1888, noted in a speech the account of a newspaper reporter who had disguised himself as "a decent laborer" and attended services at several prominent churches in an unnamed American city. In some of them he was greeted with "cold politeness," while in others he was shown "positive rudeness." In only one or two was he given a cordial welcome, and even then there was surprise to see him. The evidence was undeniable, McCosh believed, that many Christians preferred to practice their charity at a distance. "You who sit in these cushioned pews put money in the plate to send the gospel to Timbuktu," he said. "Do you send it to that man who lives next door to you?"[86] That theme was picked up years later by one of McCosh's successors at Princeton, Woodrow Wilson. "I believe that the churches of this country, at any rate the Protestant churches, have dissociated themselves from the people of this country," he said in a speech in 1901. "They are serving the classes and they are not serving the masses. They serve certain strata, certain uplifted strata, but they are not serving the men whose need is dire. The churches have more regard to their pew rents than to the souls of men."[87]

George Marsden comments that Wilson's struggles to curb the elitism at Princeton were symptomatic of the struggles of mainstream Protestantism as a whole during that era. The churches, he writes, "were running up against the realities of rapidly increasing wealth within their own constituency."[88] Although Washington Gladden, Josiah Strong, and others were already, at the time of the Briggs trials, laying the foundations of what would become, during the next generation, the social gospel movement, at that point they were working pretty much alone. "We were few and we shouted in the wilderness," said Walter Rauschenbusch.[89]

---

[86]Cited in Carter, *Spiritual Crisis*, 140.

[87]Cited in Marsden, *The Soul of the American University*, 230.

[88]Ibid., 228. H. Richard Niebuhr makes the same point in *Social Sources of Denominationalism* (see 150-51 and 161), as does Arthur Schlesinger in *A Critical Period in American Religion* (14-15).

[89]Quoted in Schlesinger, *A Critical Period in American Religion*, 26.

It was probably too much to expect the son of New York's barrel king to have endorsed a movement that so overtly championed the cause of labor. Briggs's preferred vehicle for reform was the Salvation Army. But even there, his writings on the subject seem distracted and disengaged,[90] an attitude toward political issues that seems to have been consistent throughout his adult life. Historian Mark Massa notes that while Briggs was in the Civil War (he had a brief, uneventful career as a Union soldier), his letters reveal "an earnest young Christian totally uninvolved in either the ethical questions of slavery or the larger course of the war." In one letter, Briggs urged his sister, "Do not let the present excitements distract you from the one thing necessary"—conversion to Christ.[91] When Union Seminary began adding courses related to the social gospel in 1899, the initiative was spearheaded by another, younger professor; Briggs by then was busy with his plans to turn Union into a university.[92] The bulk of his energies, however, were devoted to the international ecumenical movement, which he clearly saw as a vehicle to further his obsessions with the promulgation of historical criticism and the overthrow of "traditionalists and dogmaticians" in the church.[93]

Some Comments on the Limits of Technique

During his long heresy ordeal, Briggs's confidence in himself and in his views never seemed to falter. Indeed, in virtually every proceeding in which he was allowed to give a presentation, he gave better than he got.[94] No doubt this remarkable sense of resolution can be credited to some degree to a naturally stubborn and argumentative nature, but it also rested on the unshakable social position he enjoyed as a "gentleman and a scholar." To those

---

[90]See Charles Briggs, "The Salvation Army," *The North American Review* 159/6 (December 1894): 697-710.

[91]Massa, *Charles Augustus Briggs*, 28.

[92]Handy, *Union Theological Seminary*, 106.

[93]See Massa, *Charles Augustus Briggs*, chap. 5; and Christensen, *The Ecumenical Orthodoxy of Charles Augustus Briggs*, passim.

[94]The newspaper articles collected by Thomas Hastings often ran lengthy summaries or verbatim accounts of Briggs's statements during his trials, as well as of the statements of his opponents.

prerogatives Briggs added a third, newer source of entitlement: the power of technique.[95]

I noted earlier that Briggs and his supporters were as excited by the revolutionary potential of historical criticism as others were about the telephone or the light bulb. The technical kinship criticism shared with those inventions was no coincidence. Indeed, it explains why historical criticism arose and overtook hermeneutics when it did. Criticism is a technique, and as such it fit perfectly with a world in which technique was rapidly becoming an overwhelming, all-encompassing force. Charles Mabee, following Jacques Ellul, has defined "technique" as "an autonomous methodological approach to the world that intends to adapt us more completely to the rationality of the machine. . . . "[96] A key element of technique is its drive to break down all relationships, ideas, and activities into efficient, *systematic* components. Anything that does not comfortably fit into the parameters of the system in question is considered, in the technological worldview, as alien and a threat.

The Bible, of course, was ancient, contradictory, illogical, filled with emotion and mystery—all anathema to the demands of technique. For Briggs, criticism offered a means of clearing that confusion away: beneath the Bible's unruly surface, he believed, a divine order could be discerned which was logical, precise, and, above all, consistent. Like the assembly line, historical criticism was portrayed by Briggs and others as an objective technique that would efficiently produce superior results. Theologically, it was neutral: the displacement of traditional methods, assumptions, and beliefs was only a byproduct of the critical method, but a necessary one.[97] Traditional views of the Bible stood in the way of historical criticism (recall Briggs's six "obstacles" to biblical faith) and had to be

---

[95]That a member of the Protestant establishment should hold progressive ideas, at least as regards the advantages of technological progress, might seem contradictory at first, but in fact makes perfect sense. It was the privileged classes who were in the best position to capitalize on the new opportunities offered by the emerging technologies, which required huge capital investments. The enthusiastic endorsement by men of Briggs's standing was a matter of simple self-interest: their privilege stood to be enhanced.

[96]Mabee, *Reading Sacred Texts*, 24.

[97]Mabee quotes Lewis Mumford on how capitalism has exploited the supposed neutrality of technique. See Mabee's *Reading Sacred Texts*, 48.

removed, much as a forest must be cleared to make way for development.

The irony was that while Briggs believed he was employing criticism as a technique, in truth technique was employing him. The irresistible power of technique to absorb those who would use it is a central theme in the writings of Jacques Ellul, who describes how technique "desacralizes" the world:

> For technique nothing is sacred, there is no mystery, no taboo.
> . . . Technique worships nothing, respects nothing. It has a single role: to strip off externals, to bring everything to light, and by rational use to transform everything into means. More than science, which limits itself to explaining the "how," technique desacralizes because it demonstrates (by evidence and not by reason, through use and not through books) that mystery does not exist. Science brings to the light of day everything man had believed sacred. Technique takes possession of it and enslaves it. The sacred cannot resist. . . . The mysterious is merely that which has not yet been technicized.[98]

This helps explain why Briggs went to such lengths in his inaugural address to play down the miracles in the Bible: he needed to "technicize" the mysterious.[99] The church, he argued, had severely overplayed miracle as a component of biblical revelation, which was one of the main reasons "men" of science could not take the Bible seriously. In truth, according to Briggs, ever so often God had used a miracle as an act of redemption to help out someone who really needed it—that was the extent of it. "[T]here is no reason," Briggs said, "why we should claim that [the

---

[98]This passage, from Ellul's *Ethics of Freedom*, is quoted by Mabee in *Reading Sacred Texts*, 74-75. Ellul himself lays out the essence of his views on technique in *The Technological Society* (New York: Alfred A. Knopf) 1967. Also see Ellul's *The Technological Bluff* (Grand Rapids MI: Eerdmans) 1990.

[99]It is clear from reading Albert Schweitzer's overview of early biblical criticism that the problem of rationalizing miracles has been fundamental to the critical task from its outset. See *The Quest of the Historical Jesus: A Critical Study of Is Progress from Reimarus to Wrede*, trans. William Montgomery (repr.: New York: Macmillan, 1948; [1910]). Also see William C. Placher, *The Domestication of Transcendence: How Modern Thinking about God Went Wrong* (Louisville KY: Westminster/John Knox Press, 1996).

Bible's miracles] in any way violate the laws of nature or disturb its harmonies."[100]

When miracle is sacrificed for mechanics, the danger is that the Spirit will also get lost. Many of today's more perceptive theologians have pointed out that this is just the problem with the critical approach.[101] The traditional hermeneutical relationship between reader and scripture has been reversed: the critic exercises his or her judgment upon the text, rather than letting the text act upon him or her. Mabee cites this bias toward activity as a "basic flaw" in modern study of the Bible. "Technology tends to direct us toward outward and external realities," he writes. "Our infatuation with the external enables us to bypass the far more complex and elusive interior world of the text."[102]

That shortcoming is obvious in Briggs's exegetical commentaries. In 1906–1907, for example, his two-volume, line-by-line textual analysis of the Psalms was published.[103] This work was an invaluable contribution to biblical scholarship at the time, but for anyone who is not a textual scholar, the overall effect is stupefyingly lifeless. Here is an excerpt from Briggs's commentary on Psalm 23:

> Its structure is artistic. The three [strophes] are tetrastichs, with parallel themes: shepherd . . . guide . . . host. . . . It is a mistake to suppose that the theme of the shepherd extends into the 2d [strophe]. While it is true that the shepherd may conduct his flocks through the gloomy wadys safely, yet there is nothing in

---

[100]Briggs, *Inaugural Address*, 37.

[101]In addition to Mabee, others who have written on this point include Wesley Kort, in *"Take, Read,"* and David Lyle Jeffrey, in *People of the Book: Christian Identity and Literary Culture* (Grand Rapids MI: Eerdmans, 1996). Also see Richard B. Hays, "Salvation by Trust? Reading the Bible Faithfully," *The Christian Century* (26 February 1997): 218-23.

[102]Mabee, *Reading Sacred Texts*, 105.

[103]Charles Augustus Briggs and Emilie Grace Briggs (Briggs's daughter), *A Critical and Exegetical Commentary on the Book of Psalms*, 2 vols., International Critical Commentary 15 (Edinburgh: T. & T. Clark; New York: Charles Scribner's Sons, 1906–1907). See also Charles Augustus Briggs, *The Ethical Teaching of Jesus* (New York: Scribner's, 1904); and *The Incarnation of the Lord. A Series of Sermons Tracing the Unfolding of the Doctrine of the Incarnation in the New Testament* (New York: Scribner's, 1902).

> any terms used to suggest a flock. . . . [Strophe 2] is a progressive
> tetrameter tetrastich with a cæsura in each line. The guide takes
> the place of the shepherd in a parallel conception.[104]

Briggs was quite capable of writing for a popular audience, as he
demonstrated in *Whither?* and in *The Ethical Teaching of Jesus*,
published in 1904. He was not capable, it appears, of homiletic
inspiration. In neither book did he succeed in demonstrating that
"true and higher harmony" he had promised historical criticism
would reveal.

Nor was Briggs personally a good advertisement for the
spiritual benefits historical criticism had to offer. Despite the
"affable and courteous manner" described by the *New York World*,
what consistently comes across in Briggs's books, articles, and
addresses is an unpleasant air of arrogance, defensiveness, pride,
judgment, and combativeness.

Apparently, Briggs was no more cordial to his students than he
was to his opponents in the church. Historian Robert T. Handy
quotes a Union student who wrote that although most of his
fellows endorsed the principles of higher criticism, none of them
liked Briggs very much. "In fact he is no teacher," the student said.
"You must ask questions and even when you do that he seems to
antagonize you."[105]

As noted above, Briggs's talent for provocation played a significant role in creating a "panic" over the threat historical criticism
posed for traditional beliefs. He was hardly the first critical scholar
to have run up against traditional sensibilities regarding the Bible,
nor would he be the last. No doubt historical criticism attracts
personalities who relish such confrontations. From David Friedrich
Strauss to the Jesus Seminar, the harsh disrespectfulness with
which critical views have often been presented has helped create
an emotional backlash that has influenced the way such views
have been received.[106] There is more to this pattern, however, than

---

[104]Briggs and Briggs, *The Book of Psalms*, 1:207-209.
[105]Handy, *Union Theological Seminary*, 91.
[106]This is another theme that surfaces throughout Schweitzer's *Quest of the
Historical Jesus*. Even Schweitzer's English translator in 1910 felt compelled, in a
prefatory note, to apologize for the spirit of "hate" which characterized many of

simply bad manners or bad politics. It speaks to the inherent imperialism of technique.

Wesley Kort and Stanley Fish have pointed out that knowledge, as a source of power in modern culture, is often hoarded or wielded violently; language reminiscent of rape is not uncommon.[107] At several points in Briggs's inaugural address the undertones of lust and conquest were startlingly clear. At one point, he said that

> Higher Criticism has forced its way into the Bible itself and brought us face to face with the holy contents so that we may see and know whether they are divine or not. . . .
> . . . Here in the citadel of the Bible two hosts confront the most sacred things of our religion—the one, the defenders of traditionalism, trembling for the ark of God; the other, the critics, a victorious army, determined to capture all its sacred treasures and to enjoy all its heavenly glories.[108]

Charles Mabee says that in times of chaos, when old belief systems are crumbling, cultures are attracted to new absolutes. Briggs became what Mabee calls a "priest of regimentation," offering Higher Criticism as the technology of rescue. "The new philosophy was strong precisely where the culture was weak, . . . " Mabee writes. "Indeed, the old faith could survive in vital form only if it sold its soul to mechanical messianism."[109]

The final verdict on Briggs, it seems to me, is that he was guilty of inflicting ecological damage on the community of faith. One can appreciate the exhilaration he must have felt in discover-

---

the critical works Schweitzer examined. "We are not accustomed," he wrote, "to be so ruthless in England." See *Quest*, v. As for the Jesus Seminar, American newspapers have for years feasted on the controversy provoked by the seminar's colorful sessions, particularly because of its practice (technique) of voting Yea or Nay on the authenticity of various New Testament passages by the casting of colored balls. For an overview and rebuttal, see Luke Timothy Johnson, *The Real Jesus: The Misguided Quest for the Historical Jesus and the Truth of the Traditional Gospels* (San Francisco: HarperCollins, 1996).

[107]Kort, "*Take, Read*," 99.

[108]Briggs, *Inaugural Address*, 34, 41. Briggs used the word "force" at least five times in the course of this address, each time in a similar manner.

[109]Mabee, *Reading Sacred Texts*, 50.

ing the insights historical criticism had to offer; and one can admire his determination that this new knowledge had to be absorbed by the "mind" of the church. It is also important to acknowledge how constricting traditional dogma must have seemed at the time; nostalgia for a simpler, clearer religious environment overlooks how crushing and unjust doctrinal uniformity has frequently been. Nonetheless, it is fair to say that Briggs could have been more cognizant of the destructive potential of critical technique, and more willing to accept his concomitant responsibility to handle it with due respect for the environment in which he worked. If there was a hunger in the late nineteenth century for reassurance amidst tumultuous change, Briggs never acknowledged the validity of his opponents' fears that criticism was undercutting traditional sources of spiritual sustenance. Nor was he able to offer a satisfying alternative vision.

It would not be fair to expect Briggs to transcend the limits of criticism were it not for the fact that he aspired so aggressively to do just that. Alas, academic expertise is not the same as spiritual or moral leadership. In his zeal to guide mainstream Protestantism into the modern era, Briggs overreached his capacities, and overestimated the spiritual powers and psychosocial dynamics of historical criticism. He was far from alone in that error: the limits of scholarship, science, and technology had not yet been appreciated. They still aren't, much of the time.

The ultimate irony, of course, was that Briggs, like many technocrats, discovered too late that the machine he had cranked up was no longer in his control. When one of his successors began applying critical methods to the gospel accounts of the virgin birth and the resurrection, Briggs lobbied for his dismissal.[110] Briggs learned the lesson many of us in the late twentieth century now take for granted: Technique is fine, up to a point. But it always wants to go too far, and at the same time never goes far enough.

---

[110]Massa, *Charles Augustus Briggs*, 151.

The Body as Reader
African-Americans, Freedom, and the American Myth

Kimberleigh Jordan

The United States of America understands itself to be a nation conceived in liberty and freedom. From the beginning of the European migration and initial construction of the American myth to the present, freedom and liberty have been defining themes of the rhetoric of "America." Consider the national anthem that declares this the "land of the free and the home of the brave" and the pledge of allegiance that asserts "liberty and justice for all." Consider, too, the sentiments of a Country and Western song which experienced a resurgence during the Gulf War: "I'm proud to be an American, where *at least* I know I'm free."[1] Proclamations of patriotism herald freedom and liberty as the sine qua non of the American experience.

As a descendant of Africans who were kidnapped into North America chattel enslavement, I find these themes of freedom and justice, both implicit and explicit in the American myth, rather hollow for people of African descent. Even those African-Americans who buy into the myth find numerous problems and contradictions along their journey toward perceived American freedom. Rather than finding the freedom and liberty that the Pilgrims and Puritans understood as ordained for them, enslaved Africans and their descendants have experienced varying degrees of "un-freedom." There is a bitter irony in the long history of various modes of captivity—physical, psychological, spiritual, economic—of

---

[1] "God Bless the U.S.A." by Lee Greenwood.

African peoples in America, a society that defines itself in terms of the quest for liberty and justice.

With various types of bondage and resistances as enduring experiences of African peoples in the United States, the notion of freedom and liberty *for all* as constitutive of the American myth, must be reexamined.[2] The myth reflects what Swedish social scientist Gunnar Myrdal called "the American dilemma"—the conflict between high-sounding Christian and Enlightenment concepts and ideals on the one hand and the actual structure of power relations on the other.[3] The discrepancy between the two poles of this American dilemma, and some of the cultural formations that reflect it, will be the focus of this essay. African-Americans, and African-American women most acutely, find themselves on the distant

---

[2]The following excerpts are from civic documents that are among the sacred planks of the myth of America.

The Declaration of Independence. "We hold these truths to be self evident, that all men are created equal, that they are endowed by their Creator with certain unalienable rights, that among these are Life, Liberty, and the pursuit of Happiness. That to secure these rights, Governments are instituted among Men, deriving their just powers from the consent of the governed. That whenever any Form of Government becomes destructive of these ends, it is the Right of the People to alter or to abolish it, and to institute new Government, laying its foundation on such principles and organizing its powers in such form, as to them shall seem most likely to effect their Safety and Happiness."

The Preamble to the Constitution. "WE THE PEOPLE of the United States, in Order to form a more perfect Union, establish Justice, insure domestic Tranquility, provide for the common defence, promote the general Welfare, and secure the Blessings of Liberty to ourselves and our Posterity, do ordain and establish this Constitution for the United States of America. . . . "

Excerpts from the Reconstruction Amendments:

Amendment XIII. Section 1. "Neither slavery nor involuntary servitude, except as a punishment for crime whereof the party shall have been duly convicted, shall exist within the United States, or any place subject to their jurisdiction. . . . "

Amendment XIV. Section 1. " . . . No State shall make or enforce any law which shall abridge the privileges or immunities of citizens of the United States; nor shall any State deprive any person of life, liberty, or property, without due process of law; nor to deny to any person within its jurisdiction the equal protection of the laws. . . . "

Amendment XV. Section 1. "The right of citizens of the United States to vote shall not be denied or abridged by the United States or by any State on account of race, color, or previous condition of servitude.

[3]C. Eric Lincoln, *Race, Religion, and the Continuing American Dilemma* (New York: Hill and Wang, 1984; rev. ed., 1999) xiv.

opposite end of the experience of freedom and expansive opportunity enjoyed by elite white males, the original spinners and continuing primary beneficiaries of the American myth.

The actual *physical* location of the reader can also reflect one's experience of freedom and liberty. Where one's body is and how it is oriented serves as a canvas for learning. Therefore, in this essay the body will serve as a primary means of knowing and understanding freedom.

The American Myth

The American myth is informed and structured by at least two major streams of tradition: (1) the Bible or at least certain biblical texts; and (2) civil documents containing (according to Myrdal) "high sounding Christian concepts" that uphold notions of freedom and liberty. A poignant and dramatic argument for the Bible as cultural-foundation text is reflected in a speech by Solomon Schecter at the dedication of—of all things—the newly constructed campus of the Jewish Theological Seminary of America in 1903:

> This country is, as everybody knows, a creation of the Bible, particularly the Old Testament, and the Bible is still holding its own, exercising enormous influence as a real spiritual power in spite of all the destructive tendencies, mostly of foreign make. . . . The bulk of the real American people have, in matters of religion, retained their sobriety and loyal adherence to the Scripture, as their Puritan forefathers did.[4]

The Constitution and its subsequent amendments have also been heralded through the centuries as the legal foundation and framework of American liberty. The preamble to the Constitution sets forth the purpose, major ideas, and philosophies presented in the rest of the document. A primary objective of the Constitution is to "secure the Blessings of Liberty to ourselves and our Posterity." The general rhetoric of the American myth conveys a sense of the *universal* scope of liberty and opportunity that this primary

---

[4]Solomon Schecter, *Seminary Addresses and Other Papers*, with intro. by Louis Finkelstein (Cincinnati: Ark Pub. Co., 1915) 48-49, as quoted in Martin E. Marty, *Religion and Republic: The American Circumstance* (Boston: Beacon Press, 1987) 155.

document of American freedom actually does not support.[5] In reading the Constitution more carefully, however, one sees that "ourselves" referred only to a narrow slice of the population—white males. The later amendments to the Constitution clearly address the elitism and discrimination that haunt the original document: the thirteenth, fourteenth, and fifteenth amendments brought the newly emancipated African males closer to civic freedom; the nineteenth amendment empowered women to a greater degree. The significant part of the deliberation of higher courts today revolves around the question of who is included in the freedoms thought to be guaranteed in the Constitution.

The Bible as a Foundation of America

Two events of great historical significance took place in 1787 Philadelphia, as the rhetorical and ideological mold was being poured for the foundation of "America." The first was the Constitutional Convention that led to the signing of the U.S. Constitution. The other was the departure of Richard Allen and a group of free African Methodists from a segregated congregation after the Africans—according to the lore—were pulled from their knees because they dared to pray before the last white person had done so. In a sense, the free Africans *em-bodied* their own "declaration of independence" from white ecclesiastical oppression.[6] Bishop Reverdy Ransom, in his 1946 "Address to the Extra Session of the African Methodist Episcopal Conference," said:

As the first lines of the bill proclaiming independence for the United Colonies from Great Britain were struck off, we too,

---

[5]Elaine R. Jones, Director-Counsel of the NAACP Legal Defense Fund, notes that though the U.S. Constitution does not use the word "slavery," the word "property," which could include humans, is referenced ten times. Jones says that the framers of the constitution "enshrined slavery." Elaine R. Jones, "Race and American Institutions," The Jack and Lewis Rudin Lectures at Auburn Theological Seminary, James Chapel, Union Theological Seminary, New York City, April 30, 1997.

[6]See Lincoln, *Race, Religion, and the Continuing American Dilemma*, 57.

floated our flag six blocks away for manhood, and independence
to the establishment of a Church to the glory of God.[7]

Both the Constitutional Convention and the Africans' departure
of protest were conditioned by particular understandings on the
part of the respective groups regarding God's desire for their freedom. The unbonded Africans saw freedom as an inherent part of
their Christian journey. Their perambulatory response was a reply
to the violation of this divinely ordained freedom at the hands of
the white Methodists. This vision of spiritual equality has been
called the essence of African Methodism,[8] while also reflecting
deep, emotional sentiments and yearnings of the larger community
of enslaved and oppressed Africans. Such sentiment is reflected in
a deposition against Denmark Vesey, a leader of slave revolt in
Charleston, South Carolina in 1822:

> His general conversation was about religion which he would
> apply to slavery, as for instance, he would speak of the creation
> of the world, in which he would say all men had equal rights,
> blacks as well as whites. . . .[9]

Historian of Religion Charles Long has made the point that the
enslaved Africans brought no "text" to North America other than
their bodies. The experience with the Bible began as something
that was read to them by their oppressors. The meaning of their
experience was discerned through conjuring, divination, and their
embodied reality in connection with the stories of the Bible that
were heard. This was a use of the Bible that the enslavers were
unable to know.[10]

---

[7]In George A. Singleton, *The Romance of African Methodism: A Study of the African Methodist Episcopal Church* (New York: Exposition Press, 1952; repr.: Nashville: AME Press, 1985) 177, as quoted in Peter J. Paris, *The Social Teaching of the Black Churches* (Philadelphia: Fortress, 1985) 107.

[8]James T. Campbell, *Songs of Zion: The African Methodist Episcopal Church in the United States and South Africa* (New York: Oxford University Press, 1995; repr.: Chapel Hill: University of North Carolina Press, 1998) 24.

[9]Albert J. Raboteau, *Slave Religion: The "Invisible Institution" in the Antebellum South* (New York: Oxford University Press, 1978) 163.

[10]Charles Long's remarks were made as a panelist for "African-Americans and the Bible," a special (joint) session (S125/A150) of the American Academy of Religion and the Society of Biblical Literature, at the 1997 Annual Meeting, San

White-Protestant-American culture has generally understood the phenomenon of engaging the sacred in much narrower terms. It has circumscribed communion with the sacred in terms of the text. And it has further delineated for the whole culture what text should be read and how it should be read. It has developed a particular reading of the Bible and national documents to support the construction of a myth of America that has allowed *freedom for some.*

Interpretative Models

With these particular polar readings of the Bible in mind, I have isolated two "reading" models as vantage points from which to view the American myth. I shall argue that the Abraham story in the book of Genesis has resonated with the experiences of those in dominant positions, especially of white men, while the story of Hagar, the African *slave woman* in Genesis[11] has resonated with the dominated, including Black people, and particularly Black women.

As for Abraham and his body, his physical self, God's direction to Abraham to "go . . . ," with a promise of land and nationhood, is an example of (that) one group's understanding of divinely ordained physical liberty to move freely and without hesitation to take and inhabit land. In contrast, God's direction to Hagar, "return . . . and submit," exemplifies some physical experiences of Black women, who have been enslaved and otherwise unable to be fully free human agents of their own bodies. Hagar's ultimate survival against oppressive forces is important.

Abrahamic Model: "Go to the place I will show you"

[1]Now the Lord said to Abram, "Go from your country and your kindred and your father's house to the land that I will show you. [2]I will make of you a great nation, and I will bless you, and make

---

Francisco, 23 November 1997.

[11]See Delores S. Williams, *Sisters in the Wilderness: The Challenge of Womanist God-Talk* (Maryknoll NY: Orbis, 1993); and Renita J. Weems, "Reading Her Way through the Struggle: African-American Women and the Bible," in *Stony the Road We Trod: African-American Biblical Interpretation,* ed. Cain Hope Felder (Minneapolis: Fortress Press, 1991) 75-76.

your name great, so that you will be a blessing. [3]I will bless those who bless you, and the one who curses you I will curse; . . . " (Genesis 12:1-3a NRSV)

The Abrahamic model is implicit in the Christian myth and the American myth. Furthermore, it was constructive of the historical European quest for the so-called "new world." God tells Abraham that if he responds affirmatively to God's request he will receive land, nationhood, and God's favor. God impels him to move into unknown territory that God will provide. After hearing this call, Abraham goes forth as full and complete agent of his physical self with a promise that he will be a property owner and progenitor of generations.

The importance of property is clear. It is consonant with freedom, liberty, and property as enshrined by the framers of the United States Constitution. In the preconstitutional American era, Rev. John Cotton, a leading seventeenth-century Puritan minister, argued the freedom to take and occupy land in North America and turn it to the purpose of his group, saying:

> [W]here there is a vacant place, there is liberty for the son of Adam or Noah to come and inhabit, though they neither buy it, nor ask their leaves. . . . In a vacant soil, he taketh possession of it, and bestoweth culture and husbandry upon it, his right it is.[12]

This understanding of the American myth is legitimized by a certain reading of the Abrahamic myth in Genesis, a reading that inspired the European settlers to think that, as with Abraham, God was intimately involved with them, ordaining their affairs and ordering their movement into their "new world."[13] Although it is clear that within a certain site of interpretation what Abraham represents can be and in fact has generally been understood in terms of the marginal or exilic figure, it should be acknowledged that even as wandering figure of exile his situation is different from—an advantage over—others in the same larger story. His

---

[12]Rev. John Cotton, quoted in Charles M. Segal and David C. Stinebeck, *Puritans, Indians, and Manifest Destiny* (New York: Putnam, 1977) 31.

[13]Peter Lockwood Rumsey, "Acts of God: The Rhetoric of Providence in New England, 1620–1730" (Ph.D. diss., Columbia University, 1984) ii.

relationships with others, and the different sets of relationships that are described in the larger story, make it clear that we have to do with a far more complex situation and set of relationships and agenda than has been argued in scholarship. What is reflected in the story is a culture of the superior over the inferior, or, in the Black folk-church vernacular, "big 'I's'" and "little 'yous,' " even within the larger biblical world of "little 'yous.' " In the biblical world perspective and according to the Abrahamic model, the "big 'I's'" are the ones who have the name, the land, and the nation.

Hagar Model: "Return . . . and submit"

16:3So, after Abram had lived ten years in the land of Canaan, Sarai, Abram's wife, took Hagar the Egyptian, her *slave-girl*, and gave her to her husband Abram as a wife. 4He went in to Hagar, and she conceived; and when she saw that she had conceived, she looked with contempt on her mistress. 5Then Sarai said to Abram, "May the wrong done to me be on you! . . . May the LORD judge between you and me!" 6But Abram said to Sarai, "Your *slave-girl* is in your power; do to her as you please.' Then Sarai dealt harshly with her, and she ran away from her.
7The angel of the LORD found her by a spring of water in the wilderness, . . . 9[and] said to her, "Return to your mistress, and submit to her." . . .
15Hagar bore Abram a son; and Abram named his son, whom Hagar bore, Ishmael. (Genesis 16:3-7, 9, 15 NRSV; emphasis added)

21:10So [Sarah] said to Abraham, "Cast out this *slave woman* with her son; . . . 12But God said to Abraham, " . . . As for the son of the *slave woman*, I will make a nation of him also, because he is your offspring." . . . 14"And [Hagar] departed, and wandered about in the wilderness of Beer-sheba. . . .
. . . 19Then God opened [Hagar's] eyes and she saw a well of water. She went, and filled the skin with water, and gave the boy a drink.
20God was with the boy, and he grew up; . . . 21[and] lived in the wilderness of Paran; and his mother got a wife for him from

the land of Egypt. (Genesis 21:10, 12, 14c, 19, 20-21 NRSV; emphasis added)[14]

The experience of Hagar strikes a chord with the reality of African-American people, especially African-American women. Hagar's ordeal of enslavement, resistance, and the experience in the wilderness is analogous to the history of Black people in the United States. While attempting to run to freedom, Hagar meets a divine messenger. After the angel offers Hagar a hopeful promise, God compels her—unlike Abraham—to return and submit to her owners. In a later scene, Sarah, through Abraham, sends Hagar into the wilderness where she encounters God again. This time the deity provides sustenance for her family's survival, although her liberty and freedom are consistently limited. It is only in the spiritual realm, through her encounter and relationship with God, that she finds some freedom and the ability to survive.

Various Understandings of the Hagar Story

Readers of the Bible have appreciated Hagar over the centuries. The relationship of the reader to Hagar may depend on his or her relationship to embodied power. In my own perusal of Euro-American scholarship on the Hagar narratives, Hagar is often unmentioned or serves as a literary pawn in the larger, seemingly more important, tale of God's covenant with Abraham.

Reformers Martin Luther and John Calvin are examples of this reading of the Hagar stories. Like Paul before them,[15] Hagar's condition of enslavement is not a problem for Luther or Calvin. Also, like Paul, Calvin uses Hagar and Sarah as allegorical props to

---

[14]This translation is from the New Revised Standard Version (NRSV). Discrepancies among the English translations should be noted. In Genesis 16:3, 6, Hagar is variously a "maid" (King James Version KJV: "*hand*maid" at 16:1), a "maidservant" and simply "servant" (New International Version NIV), or a "slave-girl" (NRSV). In Genesis 21:10 both the NRSV and NIV refer to Hagar as a "slave woman" while the KJV uses the synonym "bondwoman." Both KJV and NRSV use the same terms in Genesis 21:12 as in vs. 10, but NIV returns to the term used in Genesis 16, "maidservant." These variations are important because the KJV and NIV are widely read translations among African-American churchwomen.

[15]Cf. Galatians 4:24-26 for the Apostle Paul's allegory of slavery and freedom, referencing Hagar and Sarah.

represent the church's relationship to "doctrine": Hagar represents bondage through the church's legalistic enslavement to doctrine, while Sarah represents freedom through the church's evangelical connection.[16]

Luther sees the story of Abraham and Sarah as an "example and instruction" to "all believers," though Hagar serves a minor and negative role.[17] He describes Hagar as "an example of the carnal human being who cannot be improved either by chastisement or by kindness. She is puffed up by the kind acts of her mistress."[18]

In twentieth-century European, particularly British and German culture, Hagar is also a marginalized figure. Below is a description from a fairly contemporary writer:

> Hagar, for her part, was nothing more than Sarah's property. Her only title . . . [is] slave. Her whole purpose in life was to be of service to her mistress. . . . Hagar did not belong to herself . . . [her will] had little significance . . . and her works and achievements all belonged to Sarah, her mistress.[19]

In stark contrast, within the African-American community Hagar has been held up as a figure consonant with the general experience of Black people in North America. An early indication of this appropriation is in the popularity of the name "Hagar" for baby girls in nineteenth-century enslaved communities. Further appropriation of Hagar can be seen in nineteenth-century literary traditions. Frances E. W. Harper, a noted abolitionist, lecturer, and political thinker, wrote *Iola Leroy* in 1892, which featured a character named Hagar. And Paul Laurence Dunbar created a poetic work entitled "The Afro-American Sons of Hagar Social Club."

---

[16]John Calvin, *Commentaries on the Epistles of Paul to the Galatians and Ephesians*, trans. William Pringle (Grand Rapids MI: Eerdmans, 1948) 137, as quoted in Anastasia Malle, "Hagar Names God: A Woman's Vision Arising in the Midst of Pain: Genesis 16 and 21" (S.T.M. thesis, Wartburg Theological Seminary, 1992) 25.

[17]*Luther's Works*, ed. Jaroslav Pelikan, vol. 3 (St Louis: Concordia, 1964) 52, as quoted in Malle, "Hagar Names God," 29.

[18]*Luther's Works* 3:60.

[19]Angel Gonzalez Nuncy, *Abraham: Father of Believers*, trans. Robert J. Olsen (New York: Herder and Herder, 1967) 68.

On the twentieth century literary scene, the Hagar story has continued to strike a chord. Toni Morrison features a wisewoman character named Hagar in *Song of Solomon* (1977). The first chapter of sociologist E. Franklin Frazier's *The Negro Family in the United States* is entitled "Hagar and Her Children." And the ethnographer John Langston Gwaltney calls "Aunt Hagar" a "mythical apical figure of the core Black nation."[20]

The difference between these cultural understandings of Hagar represent two different American perspectives—those for whom America represents part of the same covenant God made with Abraham, on the one hand, and those relentlessly fixed on the margins of power, on the other. These different perspectives also represent different ways of knowing freedom. African-Americans have read themselves in the experiences of Hagar and her condition of *un*freedom. Conversely, those in positions of socio-political, cultural, and economic power, in which freedom is the norm, have on the whole, read themselves in Abraham's adventurous story as a free man.

My Body as Reader

As a choreographer and dancer, I have chosen to add my body and my artistic voice to earlier forms of interpretation of the story: Hagar is a model of resistance who resonates throughout the ages. The dance presentation entitled "God Had Something in It" originally premiered on 4 April 1997 in a liturgy at the Riverside Church in New York City. I conceived of the work as an abstract artistic conversation involving dance, music, the spoken word, and the biblical text. I chose the Hagar story as focus because: (1) Hagar is identified as a woman of African descent in the Bible; (2) she was locked into a system of slavery that did not allow her

---

[20]See Delores S. Williams, *Sisters in the Wilderness*, 245n.2; and Delores S. Williams, "A Womanist Theological Approach to the Bible with Special Reference to the Hagar-Sarah Stories in Genesis," lecture, Union Theological Seminary, New York City, 5 October 1994; see also *The Norton Anthology of African-American Literature*, Henry Louis Gates, Jr. and Nellie Y. McKay, gen. eds. (New York: W. W. Norton, 1997, ©1996) s.v. "F. E. W. Harper" and "Toni Morrison"; John Langston Gwaltney, *Drylongso: A Self-Portrait of Black America* (New York: Random House, 1980; repr.: New York: New Press, 1993) xv.

agency over her own body; and (3) she had a profound and life-changing encounter with God. Throughout my choreographic process, I was keenly aware that Hagar could have been my great-grandmother.

To construct this interpretative "conversation" about Hagar, I invited two other artists to contribute. These other artists—a poet and a musician—represented elements of the liturgy that were familiar to worshipers. The Rev. Mariah Britton wrote a poem called "God Had Something in It" from the imagined flashback perspective of a woman in the community in which Hagar finally settled. Vince Anderson employed a gospel music tune by Richard Smallwood called "I Love the Lord" as his musical theme. Smallwood set lyrics written by Issac Watts in the nineteenth century. This is a tune with which many are familiar; however, instead of presenting it in the conventional way, he composed variations that subverted the familiarity and "sweetness" of the tune, employing cultural interpretative modes of jazz and the blues to communicate the Hagar experience musically.

In my work as dancer and choreographer, I have used various points of Hagar's biblical and contemporary stories as the foundation of the choreography. These "seeds" were distillations from Hagar/Black women's experience that included nurture, wilderness, escape, faith-reliance on God. I constructed working titles for the various dance sections in order to communicate some of my artistic priorities. These included: "Wilderness," "New Life," "Praise Dance," "Escape," "Sapphire," "Running for the Promise," and "Ring Shout."

This project sought to challenge the audience by means of interpretive dance to think about the Hagar story through the life-world of people of African descent in North America. Performed by an African-American woman, the dance provoked a more *embodied* thinking about Hagar. Thus, through the late modern world African-American body, Hagar and all she represents could be more powerfully imagined and responded to by contemporaries.

The dance also served as an artistic catalyst for the continuing construction and reconstruction of African-American identity. Nuancing Wesley Kort's argument for the sake of applying it to the experience of African-Americans, the Hagar stories become a container for some "assumptions, norms, and values" that give the world of Black women in North America certain "shapes, limits, and coloration."[21] Hagar's story, throughout its years of appropriation in the Black community, has sustained a type of resistance and survival.

African-American Women's Experience as a Resource

African-American women's experience in North America through the centuries has resonated with Hagar's experience in Genesis. It has been the consistent ordeal of African-American women to have to negotiate life on the margins. Like Hagar, African-American women have had little opportunity to be full agents of freedom. They have known unfreedom through the experience of their bodies—the Middle Passage, enslavement, rape, poor labor conditions, single parenthood, segregation, poverty, and so forth. For the most part, their lives can be seen as an embodied interpretation of Hagar.

Two nineteenth-century Hagars, Harriet (Araminta) Tubman (ca. 1820–1913) and Sojourner Truth (ca. 1797–1883), found themselves on the underside of the American myth of freedom and liberty. They were born a generation apart in the years between the ratification of the Constitution and the Emancipation Proclamation. Both Truth and Tubman were born slaves and only later in their lives escaped and became fearsome freedom fighters against American slavery. They battled above and below ground during a period when the freedoms thought to be guaranteed by the Constitution were being reshaped in response to the newly emancipated slave.

It is worth noting that these women utilized their bodily agency in the service of other Black people's freedom. After Tubman initiated her own escape from a plantation in Maryland, she realized that she had become "a stranger in a strange land" by escaping without her family. She noted that she made a "solemn

---

[21]Wesley A. Kort, *"Take, Read": Scripture, Textuality, and Cultural Practice* (University Park PA: Pennsylvania State University Press, 1996) 3.

resolution" that "I was free, and dey should be free also."[22] Tubman's "resolution" became the source of freedom for countless numbers of formerly enslaved Africans through the Underground Railroad. She also participated in the nineteenth-century abolitionist community.

Sojourner Truth lived out her embodied freedom in many ways, though history preserves her most often as an articulate itinerant abolitionist and women's suffragist. Like Hagar, Truth escaped slavery to find freedom in a distant location. As a sign of her new freedom, she changed her name from Isabella Van Wagener to Sojourner Truth.[23]

In their individual wars against enslavement, these women found themselves frequently colliding with the American myth. Once emancipation became legal in 1865, Truth and Tubman were on opposite sides of the issue of gratitude to President Lincoln for the reconstruction amendments to the Constitution. Truth focused a great deal of her energies on the Emancipation Proclamation, crediting President Lincoln with its passage. After meeting him at the White House in 1864 she published a letter in the antislavery press publicly communicating these thoughts.[24] Truth invested much for herself and other African-Americans in this new embodiment of freedom and liberty.

---

[22]Sarah Elizabeth Hopkins Bradford, *Harriet, the Moses of Her People* (New York: G. R. Lockwood & Son for the author, 1886) as quoted in Jean M. Humez, "In Search of Harriet Tubman's Spiritual Autobiography," in *This Far by Faith: Readings in African-American Women's Religious Biography*, ed. Judith Weisenfeld and Richard Newman (New York: Routledge, 1996) 255.

[23]Nell Irvin Painter, *Sojourner Truth: A Life, A Symbol* (New York: W. W. Norton, 1996) 4-5.

[24]Sojourner Truth, *Narrative of Sojourner Truth: A Bondswoman of Olden Time, with a History of Her Labors and Correspondence Drawn from Her "Book of Life"* [pp. 127-320] (Battle Creek MI: by the author, 1878); repr.: Schomberg Library of Nineteenth Century Black Women Writers [New York: Oxford University Press, 1991]) 176-81 (page references are to the Schomberg edition). In this report, Truth reports reverently on a Bible that President Lincoln showed her that was presented him by "the loyal colored people of Baltimore, as a token of respect and gratitude. July 4th, 1864." She reported that the cover bore a representation of a slave with shackles falling from him in a cotton field, stretching his hands toward President Lincoln in gratitude for his freedom. On the ground there was a scroll with the single word "Emancipation" written in large letters.

Less quixotic about Emancipation, Harriet Tubman had served the Union Army with soldiers in South Carolina. She saw for herself how, even on the Union side, freedom and liberty were not equally distributed to all. She witnessed the discrimination in salary that Black Union soldiers endured during the war. Thus, she came to believe much less in the ubiquity of liberty and blamed Lincoln for these discrepancies.[25]

Both of these nineteenth-century women, like Hagar of Genesis, knew "unfreedom" because of the experience of their bodies. Throughout their lives, though their legal condition as chattel ended, they knew only degrees of freedom. Neither Truth nor Tubman, or their historical African-American peers, knew freedom of the Abrahamic model—freedom to receive land and nationhood. Truth and Tubman died without seeing Black people, and especially Black women, achieve the full magnitude of freedom and liberty infused in the American myth.

A Contemporary Hagar

A century later, many would question whether African-Americans have achieved this full magnitude of American freedoms. In fact, some twentieth-century radical supporters of Black freedom use the term "amerika," or more descriptively, "amerikkka," to characterize the condition of freedom and liberty in Black communities.[26] One of these supporters of Black freedom is Assata Shakur, whose book, *Assata: An Autobiography*, is an illustration of the conflict between American rhetorical ideals of freedom and the lived experiences of African-American women.[27] Assata Shakur is a contemporary Hagar. She is a Black woman born in New York City, currently living in Cuba as a fugitive from the United States prison system. Before her imprisonment she was

---

[25]Painter, *Sojourner Truth: A Life, A Symbol*, 201-203.

[26]The spelling of "Amerika" in Afrocentric communities refers to the Kishwahili language, where the alphabet has no *c*. "Amerikkka" was used less often in twentieth-century radical language, but is used often in Assata Shakur's biography.

[27]Assata Shakur, *Assata: An Autobiography* (Westport CT: Lawrence Hill Books, 1987).

a college student and a stalwart activist for Pan-Africanist freedom. Because of her activities with the Black Panthers and other radical organizations in the early 1970s, Shakur was a target of the Federal Bureau of Investigation's COINTELPRO (Counterintelligence Program). Shakur was arrested and tried on an unfounded variety of federal and state crimes. She spent many years confined to prison before escaping to Cuba. Shakur sees that the struggle for freedom of Black people must be a struggle "against racism, capitalism, imperialism, and sexism."[28]

During her lengthy prison terms, she had many opportunities to analyze America's self-congratulating narratives of freedom and liberty. An evocative illustration of this is a reported incident in which a prison guard commanded Shakur, incarcerated in Middlesex County, New Jersey, to snap string beans. She asked the guard how much they would pay her for the service. When he informed her that there would be no payment, she refused, saying: "I don't work for nothing. I ain't gonna be no slave for nobody. Don't you know that slavery was outlawed?" The guard replied, "No, you're wrong. Slavery was outlawed with the exception of prisons. Slavery is legal in prisons."

This incident provoked even more sharply Assata Shakur's analysis of freedom for Black people in "amerika." She came to believe that the thirteenth amendment to the constitution abolished slavery, except "punishment for crime whereof the party shall have been duly convicted." She further notes that this incident shed light on why prisons in the United States are so well populated with Black and other people of color. She contrasts the high unemployment rates in Black neighborhoods to the situation of "full employment" for people in prison. The current prison-building agenda in the United States means that more people—disproportionate numbers of whom are Black and/or poor—will be outside the selected group of those who can claim the freedoms available to "Americans."

Assata Shakur came to reject the American myth of freedom. She, like Hagar, experienced the loss of agency over her physical self. In connection with her advocacy of full freedoms for Black

---

[28]Shakur, *Assata: An Autobiography*, 197.

people, including putting her body on the line in connection with controversial activities that remain unclear, she was imprisoned in the U.S. prison system. Convinced that freedom could not be realized at home, Shakur, like Hagar, took flight to find her freedom.

Conclusion

I believe that, even on the cusp of a new millennium, Hagar of Genesis is still an appropriate and powerful symbol that can help interpret the historical and enduring reality of African-American women. There is much evidence that many African-American women still find themselves in a wilderness, or a situation of con-strained "freedom." It could be said that the African-American community in general is still Hagar—seeking an encounter with the Divine, hoping one day to join the song from the wilderness: "I'm proud to be an American, where *at least* I know I'm free!"

In this essay, biblical studies, civics, womanist theology, and the arts have all converged to produce a multidisciplinary and cul-tural-expressive analysis. The focus upon embodied experience as the locus of cognition has been most important. The artistic focus has, I think, fostered a "conversation" between academic and artistic disciplines. Such conversation is important because it points to what the study of the Bible can become for persons like me. Most important is the fact that it can help foreground what all too often is lost on the margins—or in the wilderness.

Children of the American Myth
David Koresh, the Branch Davidians, and the American Bible

David Saul

The confrontation near Waco, Texas in 1993 between representatives of the federal government and a small religious community of Branch Davidians under the leadership of David Koresh is a conflict that begs to be understood. Agents of the Federal Bureau of Alcohol, Tobacco, and Firearms (BATF) and the Federal Bureau of Investigation (FBI) participated in one of the largest civilian law enforcement actions in U.S. history. It cost the U.S. government and taxpayers more than 100 million dollars, involved nearly 700 federal and local officials, and resulted in the deaths of four BATF officers and eighty Branch Davidians.[1] As I observed the fifty-one-day siege through the U.S. media, it became apparent that neither the general public on the one hand nor religious communities on the other respected Koresh's religious convictions. The question I raise in this essay is a basic one: Why? How should the reactions to Koresh on the part of the general populace be understood? What are the ramifications of such reactions? What do such reactions suggest about American society and culture?

Popular opinion took David Koresh for a crazy "cult" leader who had complete control over his fellow "cult" members.[2] The

---

[1]Stuart A. Wright, "Construction and Escalation of a Cult Threat: Dissecting Moral Panic and Official Reaction to the Branch Davidians," in *Armageddon in Waco: Critical Perspectives on the Branch Davidian Conflict*, ed. Stuart A. Wright (Chicago: University of Chicago Press, 1995) 75-76.

[2]"Cult," in the United States context, is a pejorative term that has come to refer to deviant religious groups. In the popular conception, "cults" have charis-

BATF, the FBI, the media, and the public at large were surprised that such a fanatical religious group existed at all. According to the FBI's report to the U.S. Department of Justice, Koresh's "religious rhetoric was so strong that [agents on the scene] could hardly interrupt him to discuss possible surrender."[3] FBI negotiators became increasingly frustrated throughout the siege with what they called Koresh's "Bible babble." Instead of finding someone who could speak his language, they constantly interrupted his "preaching" and demanded that he discuss the more important issues at hand.[4] From the FBI's report, it is obvious that these government agents were ill-prepared to negotiate with someone like Koresh. Their unwillingness to engage in theological discussions with Koresh contributed to the disaster.

It is no surprise that Stephen Carter defines our current age as a "culture of disbelief," in which there is no room in our public discourse for expressions of faith. Constructed, in part, to welcome citizens of all religious traditions or of no religious affiliation at all, American society and its governmental systems have done more to marginalize the religious than to include the nonreligious.

---

matic leaders who control their members through brainwashing, leading them to self-destructive behaviors including suicide. See Anson D. Shupe, Jr. and David G. Bromley, *The New Vigilantes: Deprogrammers, Anti-Cultists, and the New Religions*, Sage Library of Social Research 113 (Beverly Hills CA: Sage Publications, 1980); David G. Bromley and Anson D. Shupe, Jr., *Strange Gods: The Great American Cult Scare* (Boston: Beacon Press, 1981); J. Gordon Melton and Robert L. Moore, *The Cult Experience: Responding to the New Religious Pluralism* (New York: Pilgrim Press, 1982); R. Laurence Moore, *Religious Outsiders and the Making of Americans* (New York: Oxford University Press, 1986). Also see Jacob Needleman and George Baker, eds., *Understanding the New Religions* (New York: Seabury Press, 1978); Thomas Robbins, William C. Shepherd, and James McBride, eds., *Cults, Culture, and the Law: Perspectives on New Religious Movements* (Chico CA: Scholars Press, 1985); Marc Galanter, ed., *Cults and New Religious Movements* (Washington DC: American Psychiatric Association, 1989); and Aidan A. Kelly, ed., *The Evangelical Christian Anti-Cult Movement* (New York: Garland Publishing, 1990).

[3]U.S. Department of Justice, *Report to the Deputy Attorney General on the Events at Waco, Texas: February 28 to April 19, 1993* (Washington DC: GPO, 1993) 57-58.

[4]For a detailed analysis of the miscommunication between Koresh and the FBI negotiators, see James D. Tabor, "Religious Discourse and Failed Negotiations: The Dynamics of Biblical Apocalypticism in Waco," in Wright, *Armageddon*, 263-81; and Nancy T. Ammerman, "Waco, Federal Law Enforcement, and Scholars of Religion," in Wright, *Armageddon*, 282-96.

"Contemporary American politics faces few greater dilemmas than deciding how to deal with the resurgence of religious belief."[5]

Yet, many religious commentators did not dismiss Koresh as "crazy" simply because he held religious beliefs; they considered him fanatical because of the *nature* of these beliefs. Jim Wallis offers such a response, in an article in *Sojourners* entitled "Giving Religion a Bad Name." Wallis challenges Koresh's right to call himself a Christian, or even "religious," because of his biblical interpretations:

> If by "religious" we mean the authentic faith traditions from which the fanatics claim to come, then their religious fidelity can rightly be tested by those traditions. Does David Koresh, leader of Waco's Branch Davidians, remind us of the Jesus Christ who he claims to be? . . . Does amassing an arsenal of lethal weaponry and threatening the lives of countless people follow the steps of the nonviolent savior who chose the way of the cross? Does making apocalyptic predictions about the end of the world and then justifying his crazy behavior on the basis of those predictions show his obedience to the Bible, as he claims, when biblical teaching explicitly *forbids* making such predictions?
>
> David Koresh is not Jesus Christ returned; he is not even a follower of Jesus Christ. He is instead misguided, confused, paranoid, egotistical, maniacal, seemingly mean-spirited, and, above all, very dangerous.[6]

Wallis holds that the beliefs and actions of Koresh did not reflect the faith tradition from which he claimed to come. He challenges Koresh's biblical interpretations—in fact, his very competence to interpret the text. Should contemporary followers of Jesus—a first-century CE man who challenged his earthly leaders and claimed divine authority—be surprised when their fellow Christians do the same?[7]

---

[5]Stephen L. Carter, *The Culture of Disbelief: How American Law and Politics Trivialize Religious Devotion* (New York: Basic Books, 1993) 3.

[6]Jim Wallis, "Giving Religion a Bad Name," *Sojourners* (May 1993): 50.

[7]It is important to note that David Koresh never claimed to be Jesus Christ, as is popularly believed, but said he was the anointed one of God whose purpose was to open the seventh seal described in the book of Revelation. See below.

Stephen O'Leary, in *Arguing the Apocalypse*, notes how news reporters sought "to distinguish Seventh-day Adventism, a respected Christian denomination, from the bizarre teachings and practices of the Branch Davidians."[8] None of the commentators noted by O'Leary recognized that the Branch Davidians, a sect of the Seventh-day Adventists, the Millerite Movement that spawned Seventh-day Adventism, and the Christian tradition in general have always possessed apocalyptic tendencies that sacralize martyrdom and violence.[9]

Religious beliefs do play a powerful role in many Americans' lives; at the same time, the advent of powerful new communication and transportation networks has made America's religious diversity more evident. Gordon Melton and Robert Moore note that by 1982 there were more than 800 Christian denominations and another 600 non-Christian religious bodies in the United States.[10] When politicians and religious leaders in this country appeal to our "common" religious tradition, they ignore the extreme diversity within our religious (including Christian) traditions.

Nevertheless, there is indeed a powerful "American Myth" informing our society, as many American religious historians have noted. Martin Marty contends that

> if [historians] stayed around and took a little longer look in that [American] shrine they would not find it empty. In the corner, under a layer of dust, there is a leatherbound, gilt-edged, India-papered object, a Bible, revered *as* object, *as* icon, not only in Protestant churches but in much of the public congregation as well.[11]

---

[8]Stephen D. O'Leary, *Arguing the Apocalypse: A Theory of Millennial Rhetoric* (New York: Oxford University Press, 1994) 226.

[9]For a discussion of Early Christian perspectives of self-killing and martyrdom, see Arthur J. Droge and James D. Tabor, *A Noble Death: Suicide and Martyrdom Among Christians and Jews in Antiquity* (San Francisco: HarperSanFrancisco, 1992) 113-83.

[10]J. Gordon Melton and Robert L. Moore, *The Cult Experience: Responding to the New Religious Pluralism* (New York: Pilgrim Press, 1982) 7.

[11]Martin E. Marty, *Religion and Republic: The American Circumstance* (Boston: Beacon Press, 1987) 143.

While the "public congregation" has become secular, it has not rejected its cultural and religious heritage altogether, retaining the Bible as one of its authorities.

This heritage has deep roots in the European hegemony. John Winthrop, the longtime governor of the Massachusetts Bay Colony, outlined the vision for the new Puritan society in his sermon, "A Modell of Christian Charity." While traveling to the "New World" in 1630, Winthrop stated:

> We shall find that the God of Israel is among us, when ten of us shall be able to resist a thousand of our enemies, when He shall make us a praise and glory, that men shall say of succeeding plantations: the Lord make it like that of New England: for we must consider that we shall be as a City upon a Hill, the eyes of all people are upon us; so that if we shall deal falsely with our God in this work we have undertaken, and so cause him to withdraw his present help from us, we shall be made a story and a byword through the world.[12]

Charles Mabee describes the American myth as a "rhetoric of exceptionality and mission."[13] The Puritans and many other colonists believed they had been selected by God to come to the "New World" and that God had given them a mission to fulfill. Jesus' words in the Gospel of Matthew applied to them: "Ye are the light of the world. A city that is set on a hill cannot be hid" (Matthew 5:14 KJV). In this city, set apart from the "Old World" and its problems, they would model a pure and faithful Christian community dedicated to the service of God. The "New World," the "New England," was also the "New Canaan" or the "New Eden" or the "New Jerusalem": the place in which they would dedicate themselves to the "New Covenant."

---

[12]Perry Miller and T. H. Johnson, *The Puritans* (New York: American Book Co., 1938) 198-99. Spelling and punctuation have been modernized. Cf. Matthew 5:14; Psalm 46:1; 1 Kings 9:7; 2 Chronicles 7:20; Psalm 44:14.

[13]Charles Mabee, *Reimagining America: A Theological Critique of the American Mythos and Biblical Hermeneutics*, StABH 1 (Macon GA: Mercer University Press, 1985) 28.

The Puritans found the story of their lives reflected in the Bible. They were Adam and Eve, Abraham and Sarah, Moses and the children of Israel, the disciples of Jesus, and the firstfruits described in the book of Revelation. The Bible was not merely a collection of ancient books, but the word of God spoken to *them*. Perry Miller describes the Puritan's biblical hermeneutic as typological.[14] They believed that events described in the Bible foreshadowed the events to come in their own lives. If they were faithful, they would accomplish their divinely ordained mission to be a light unto all nations.

This Puritan myth quickly became the American myth as the fledgling nation claimed a mythical history. It offered the leadership of this new country a justification for its dominance over North America. In this way, the government of the United States rested both on the power of its citizenry, and on the will of God. Like all myths, this set of tenets can be understood as a text, subject to interpretation in an almost endless number of ways. Many prominent Americans, including Thomas Jefferson, Benjamin Franklin, Ralph Waldo Emerson, Henry David Thoreau, Herman Melville, Nathaniel Hawthorne, and Walt Whitman (to name a few) spent much of their careers offering reinterpretations of the old Puritan myth.[15] The power of this myth is revealed even more dramatically when one considers how America's political and social critics have used the myth's own language to promote their visions for change. Martin Luther King, Jr., for example, offered critiques of America that were all the more powerful because he wrapped them in the language of the American myth:

> I just want to do God's will. And He's allowed me to go up to the mountain. And I've looked over. And I've seen the promised

---

[14]See Perry Miller, ed., *Images or Shadows of Divine Things by Jonathan Edwards* (New Haven CT: Yale University Press, 1948) 6.

[15]See Conrad Cherry, *God's New Israel: Religious Interpretations of American Destiny* (Englewood Cliffs NJ: Prentice-Hall, 1971); David Lyle Jeffrey, *People of the Book: Christian Identity and Literary Culture* (Grand Rapids MI: Eerdman's, 1996); Mason I. Lowance, Jr., *The Language of Canaan: Metaphor and Symbol in New England from the Puritans to the Transcendentalists* (Cambridge MA: Harvard University Press, 1980); and Mabee, *Reimagining America*.

land. I may not get there with you. But I want you to know tonight, that we, as a people will get to the promised land."[16]

A plethora of faith communities and a variety of interpretations of an ambiguous text/common scripture—this is the state of (religious) affairs in the United States since the Pilgrims and other Europeans landed on North American shores. Within this environment, the Branch Davidians, like many groups before them, clashed with the government and with others who held different American mythical and biblical interpretations. Yet, almost everyone involved has drawn from the same mythical and biblical well. While interpretations may appear very different on the surface, closer consideration of the Davidian tradition and rhetoric reveals connections to widely shared American traditions. Such a study can provide the starting point for a more constructive dialogue across the American (religious) spectrum.

The Millerite, Seventh-day Adventist, and Branch Davidian Traditions

On 19 April 1993, after a fifty-one-day siege, seventy-four Branch Davidians died in a fire ignited after the FBI punched holes and inserted CS gas (a tear gas used for riot control)[17] into the Mt.

---

[16]Martin Luther King, Jr., "I See the Promised Land," in *A Testament of Hope. The Essential Writings and Speeches of Martin Luther King, Jr.*, ed. James Melvin Washington (San Francisco: Harper & Row, 1986; pbk. repr.: San Francisco: HarperSanFrancisco, 1991) 286. For a discussion of how Martin Luther King, Jr. engaged the American myth, see "The Challenge to America's Conscience," in Washington's introduction to *A Testament of Hope*, xviii-xix.

[17]Ortho-Chlorobenzylidenemalononitrile; compound #2178 in Susan Budavari, ed., *The Merck Index: An Encyclopedia of Chemicals, Drugs, and Biologicals*, 12th ed. (Whitehouse Station NJ: Merck, 1996) 354-55; possible symptoms of overexposure include burning and inflammation in the eyes, irritation of the throat, coughing, chest constriction, skin irritation and blistering, and headache. See also U.S. Department of Health and Human Services, Public Health Service, Centers for Disease Control, National Institute for Occupational Safety and Health, *NIOSH Pocket Guide to Chemical Hazards*, 90-117 (Washington DC: DHHS, 1990) 66. For discussion of the harmful effects of the gas on the children in the complex, see Alan A. Stone, *Report and Recommendations Concerning the Handling of Incidents Such as the Branch Davidian Standoff in Waco, Texas* (Washington DC: U.S. Justice Department, 1993). Further discussion of the dangers of CS gas is in Dean M. Kelley, "Waco: A Massacre and Its Aftermath," in *First Things* 53 (May 1995): 31, 34.

Carmel complex near Waco, Texas. This final action lasted more than six hours and involved two M-60 tanks and four Bradley armored vehicles. "A loudspeaker blared, 'David, you have had your fifteen minutes of fame. . . . Vernon[18] is no longer the Messiah. Leave the building now. You are under arrest. This standoff is over.' "[19]

The conflict had begun on 28 February 1993, when seventy-six heavily armed BATF officers stormed the Mount Carmel center in order to serve a single search-and-arrest warrant for the possible possession of illegal firearms. A gun battle shortly ensued; four BATF officers and six Branch Davidians were killed. In total, eighty Branch Davidians, including twenty-one children, and four BATF officers died in the course of the conflict.[20] Who fired the first shot and how the fire later began are issues still unresolved. Yet all agree this event was a terrible tragedy.

When the BATF raided their home near Waco, Texas, in 1993, there were 130 Branch Davidians living at Mount Carmel: forty-one men, forty-six women, and forty-three children.[21] The community was diverse in race, class, ethnicity, and nationality. Of the eighty Branch Davidians who died, forty-one were white, twenty-eight were black, six were Hispanic, and five were Asian. Forty-six were U.S. citizens, twenty-one were British, five were Australians, three were Filipinos, two were New Zealanders, two were Canadians, and one was Israeli.[22]

As leader, David Koresh had recruited most of the current Branch Davidians in the 1980s and 1990s, but some had lived at the Mount Carmel center since the 1950s. The overwhelming majority of the Branch Davidians were Seventh-day Adventists, the denomination Koresh sought to reform. Koresh believed, like the earlier leaders of the Branch Davidians, that the Seventh-day Adventists had strayed from their original purpose. The first focus of

---

[18]Vernon Howell was the given name of David Koresh. See below.

[19]James Tabor and Eugene V. Gallagher, *Why Waco?: Cults and the Battle for Religious Freedom in America* (Berkeley: University of California Press, 1995) 2.

[20]Wright, "Construction and Escalation," 75-76.

[21]Tabor and Gallagher, *Why Waco?*, 252-53.

[22]Wright, "Appendix. Branch Davidians Who Died at Mt. Carmel," in Wright, *Armageddon*, 379-81.

Koresh's two-stage mission was to gather a small group of the faithful; these would become the chosen martyrs of the Fifth Seal (Revelation 6:9-11); they would receive leadership roles in the coming Kingdom of God. In the second stage, Koresh "would be a general witness to the Adventist church, as a whole"; he would "prepare the way for the 144,000 worthy ones who would be spared in the coming great conflagration, as foretold in Revelation 7."[23] The Branch Davidians' goal was to purify the Seventh-day Adventists and prepare them for the imminent return of Christ. Koresh and the earlier Davidian leaders believed "they represented a theological vision that was actually more loyal to the founder [sic] William Miller and the prophet Ellen G. White than that of the apostate parent body."[24]

The history of the Seventh-day Adventists is a vital part of the Branch Davidian story.[25] In 1838 (and with the help of Joshua Himes, a fellow Baptist minister and an effective promoter), William Miller (1782–1849) began a religious movement that is now quite possibly the largest indigenous religious movement in the United States.[26] Eighty-four groups and sects would develop from the "Millerite Movement," including Seventh-day Church of God, Jehovah's Witnesses, Sacred Name groups, and the Seventh-day Adventists. (This last is by far the largest group, numbering 790,731—in 4,297 local churches—in the U.S. in 1997 and 9,296,127

---

[23]Tabor and Gallagher, *Why Waco?*, 25.

[24]Ibid., 44. Of course, Miller was the "founder" of Adventism in America insofar as his teachings and the "Millerite Movement" provided the foundation for a number of Adventist groups. Properly speaking, Joseph Bates, James White, and James's wife Ellen Gould White were the "founders" of the Seventh-day Adventist Church, and many think of the long-lived "prophet" Ellen White as the primary founder of SDA because of the extensive influence of her teachings, especially through her many writings.

[25]For useful studies on the early history of the Millerite Movement see P. Gerard Damsteegt, *Foundations of the Seventh-day Adventist Message and Mission* (Grand Rapids MI: Eerdmans, 1977); David L. Rowe, *Thunder and Trumpets: Millerites and Dissenting Religion in Upstate New York, 1800–1850* (Chico CA: Scholars Press, 1985); Ruth Alden Doan, *The Miller Heresy, Millennialism, and American Culture* (Philadelphia: Temple University Press, 1987); and Ronald L. Numbers and Jonathan M. Butler, eds., *The Disappointed: Millerism and Millenarianism in the Nineteenth Century* (Bloomington: Indiana University Press, 1987).

[26]Tabor and Gallagher, *Why Waco?*, 44.

in 207 countries worldwide at the end of 1996.) Added together these "Adventist" churches claim more than ten million members worldwide.[27]

In 1818, William Miller, a newly converted Baptist (baptized in 1816), became convinced after studying the Bible that Christ would return "about the year 1843." Miller used James Ussher's historical chronology as cited in the 1909 *Scofield Reference Bible* (King James Version) and selected Bible passages (Daniel 8:14; 9:24-27; Ezra 7:11-26) to reach this conclusion. By 1831, Miller began taking his message to the public, and by January 1844 he estimated he had given more than 4,500 lectures to more than 500,000 people in the intervening twelve years. Although many ministers and churches denounced his claims, "at the height of the Millerite fever there were probably more than 50,000 convinced believers and there may have been as many as a million others who were skeptically expectant."[28]

The year 1843 came and went without the visible return of Christ. Miller and some of his followers recalculated the date to 22 October 1844, but still nothing occurred. Yet the "Great Disappointment" did not end the Millerite movement.[29] In 1844 Hiram Edson had a vision that in that year Christ had entered the celestial holy of holies to prepare for the final judgment. Joseph Bates came to understand that the faithful must keep the seventh-day sabbath commandment, and Ellen Gould Harmon (1827–1915, originally a Methodist, and who in 1846 married one of Bates's associates, James White) received visions that confirmed both of these understandings. These new revelations and new leaders (principally Joseph Bates, James White, and Ellen Gould Harmon White) brought together various Adventist groups to form in the mid-1840s what would become the Seventh-day Adventists. The title "Seventh-day Adventist" was officially accepted in 1860; the

[27]Ibid., 224.

[28]Winthrop S. Hudson, *Religion in America. A Historical Account of the Development of American Religious Life* (New York: Charles Scribner's Sons, 1981) 197.

[29]George W. Braswell, Jr., *Understanding Sectarian Groups in America* (Nashville: Broadman, 1986) 174; Peter W. Williams, *America's Religions: Traditions and Cultures* (New York: Macmillan, 1990) 213; and Hudson, *Religion in America*, 195-97.

group was constituted on 21 May 1863, finally establishing Seventh-day Adventists as a separate denomination.

The teachings of Miller, White, and other Adventists were an important part of David Koresh's message. Miller had advocated that " 'scripture must be its own expositor' and one must not rely upon human creeds and the 'traditions of men' in arriving at the truth. . . . [A]lthough the biblical prophets used figures of speech and symbolic language to convey their message, the historical fulfillment of their words was always literal and exact."[30] Both of these interpretive principles are used by Koresh in the sermon and book he composed during the Waco siege.[31] Koresh supports every statement and answers every question he poses with a biblical reference, constantly giving historical significance to biblical metaphors. When Koresh referred to the BATF and the FBI as agents of Babylon, he was following Miller's example, who also labeled his enemies "Babylon."[32]

To many spectators, the most disturbing aspect of Koresh's teachings was his claim that he was revealing new truth. Yet this understanding came directly from Ellen White, who taught that " 'present truth' means truth for the time, which is *progressively* revealed to God's remnant people in the last days."[33] Seventh-day Adventists still accept the gift of prophecy, as their own literature attests: "[T]he Bible reveals the church's special need for divine guidance during the crisis at the time of the end; it testifies to a continuing need for and provision of the prophetic gift after New Testament times."[34] Koresh and the other Branch Davidians—like

---

[30]Tabor and Gallagher, *Why Waco?*, 45. For a detailed discussion of Miller's biblical hermeneutical principles see Damsteegt, *Foundations of the Seventh-day Adventist Message and Mission*, 16-20.

[31]See David Koresh, "A Sermon on the Seven Seals of the Book of Revelation," radio broadcast on 2 March 1993. Transcript available on web site http://www.ime.net/~mswett/march2.html and as "The Seven Seals of the Book of Revelation," in Tabor and Gallagher, *Why Waco?*, 191-203.

[32]Koresh, *Sermon* (n.p.). See below for a discussion of how Koresh uses the term "Babylon." The following discuss how Miller used the term "Babylon": Tabor and Gallagher, *Why Waco?*, 46-47, and Damsteegt, *Foundations of the Seventh-day Adventist Message and Mission*, 46-48 and 78-84.

[33]Tabor and Gallagher, *Why Waco?*, 48.

[34]*Seventh-day Adventists Believe . . . —A Biblical Exposition of 27 Fundamental Doctrines* (Washington DC: Ministerial Association, General Conference of

Miller and White before them—believed they were in the last days. In order to be faithful children of God, it was critical for them to seek the prophetic "present truth." Throughout the siege, the Seventh-day Adventists distanced themselves from Koresh and the Branch Davidians; however, the latter was clearly a sect of this denomination.

The Branch Davidians were established by Victor T. Houteff (1885–1955) in 1934. A Bulgarian immigrant who was raised Eastern Orthodox, Houteff moved to the United States in 1907. In 1918 he heard the Adventist message at a tent meeting in Rockford, Illinois, and in 1919 was baptized into the Seventh-day Adventist Church. Houteff moved to Los Angeles in 1923, and by 1929 had become active in the Olympic Exposition Park Seventh-day Adventist Church where he served as assistant superintendent of its Sabbath School. During this time he began changing the regular curriculum by teaching his own interpretation of "present truth," as related especially to Isaiah, Ezekiel, and Revelation. Eventually Houteff was denied fellowship with the local Adventist church, but he continued his new teaching and continued to gather followers.

"Convinced that the end of time was imminent, Houteff assumed two related spiritual missions"[35]: (1) to open the seven seals; and (2) to gather the 144,000 remnant who would warn the (Adventist) church of the nearing day of judgment. "The saved remnant," Houteff believed, "were soon to be transported to Palestine to establish a theocratic Kingdom of David, herald the true gospel to the world, and then ascend to heaven with the return of Christ."[36] Houteff attacked the Seventh-day Adventists for being too worldly and too institutional. He believed it was his role and the role of the Davidians to evangelize the wayward Seventh-day Adventists.

By 1934 Houteff had gathered enough followers to form an organization he called the "Shepherd's Rod" (a reference primarily

---

Seventh-day Adventists, 1988) 219.

[35]David G. Bromley and Edward D. Silver, "The Davidian Tradition: From Patronal Clan to Prophetic Movement," in Wright, *Armageddon*, 46.

[36]Ibid., 47.

to hearing the "rod," or judgment warning, of Micah 6:9 KJV). This Adventist sect accepted all of the doctrines of the Adventist tradition. These doctrines, primarily that of the "end times" (Miller) and of "Present Truth" (White), allowed the group to separate from and challenge its parent denomination. In 1935, the Shepherd's Rod group moved to a farm near Waco, Texas, which Houteff named Mt. Carmel. Although Houteff believed the group would move to Palestine within the year, Mt. Carmel became a thriving community numbering sixty-four by 1940. It became an almost self-sufficient community that produced its own food and educated its children. Houteff was a strong leader, a prophet of God in his community. He demanded separation from the world, conducted long bible studies, and led an extensive evangelism campaign directed at the Seventh-day Adventists.[37] (The Shepherd's Rod community changed its name to the Davidian Seventh-day Adventists in 1942 to avoid the draft. The "Davidian" of the name derived from Houteff's belief in the imminent restoration of David's kingdom in Palestine.)

The unthinkable happened in 1955: Victor Houteff died. This event nearly destroyed the community "because [the Davidians] had come to believe that Houteff was the new Elijah who would help usher in the reign of God."[38] Factions arose because of this crisis. However, in the November 5, 1955 issue of the Davidian monthly magazine, the *Symbolic Code*, Florence Houteff, Victor's widow, unified the Davidians by predicting that God's kingdom would be inaugurated on Passover, April 22, 1959—a prediction that Victor had refused to make. Under Florence Houteff's leadership, in the fall of 1957, the Davidians moved to another farm near Elk, nine miles east of Waco (the current site), named it New Mt. Carmel, and built new facilities. In the weeks prior to April 22, 1959, more than 1,500 faithful gathered to wait for a sign, such as the purification of the Seventh-day Adventists, the

---

[37]William L. Pitts, Jr., "Davidians and Branch Davidians: 1929–1987," in Wright, *Armageddon*, 20-30; Bromley and Silver, "The Davidian Tradition," 45-50.
[38]Pitts, "Davidians and Branch Davidians," 30.

founding of God's kingdom in Israel, or a war in the Middle East. No sign emerged for these expectant faithful.[39]

In the wake of the "second disappointment," Florence Houteff and the other Davidian officers disbanded the Davidian Association on March 11, 1962, and gave their assets to the court for disposal. Eight splinter groups emerged, and after a lengthy court battle, Benjamin Roden and his followers, the "Branch" Davidians, reclaimed the Mt. Carmel center. Resting on the Miller-White-Houteff foundation, Roden constructed a new message that initially focused on the "Branch" imagery in the Bible. The "Branch," a metaphor for both David and Christ, connected this new group with its Davidic roots and at the same time allowed it to create a separate identity. Roden instituted the observance of all Jewish festivals, continued evangelizing the Seventh-day Adventists, and strengthened his prophetic authority by claiming to be a direct descendent of David, the king of Israel.[40]

In 1977, Lois Roden, Ben Roden's wife, received in a vision the revelation that the Holy Spirit was feminine. This "present truth" provided her with the prophetic authority to assume leadership of the Branch Davidians when Ben Roden died on October 22, 1978. While Victor Houteff's unexpected death led to distress, Ben Roden's death prompted his widow to proclaim that the seventh seal had been opened. However, when nothing catastrophic occurred, various group members began to vie for leadership. Lois Roden's bitter political struggle with her son George and the controversial nature of her revelations prompted almost half of the community to leave.[41]

In 1981, the Davidians hired a handyman named Vernon Howell (he officially changed his name to David Koresh[42] in 1990), a Seventh-day Adventist from Tyler, Texas. By 1983, Lois Roden announced that Koresh would be her successor and invited all

---

[39]Ibid., 30-32; Bromley and Silver, "The Davidian Tradition," 49-50.

[40]Pitts, "Davidians and Branch Davidians," 32-35; Bromley and Silver, "The Davidian Tradition," 50-52.

[41]Pitts, "Davidians and Branch Davidians," 35-36; Bromley and Silver, "The Davidian Tradition," 51-52.

[42]"Koresh" is a transliteration of the biblical Hebrew name translated as "Cyrus"; see below.

Davidians to come and listen to his teachings. One year later, Koresh married Rachel Jones, the daughter of an influential Davidian family, strengthening his position as the next Davidian prophet. However, in 1985, George Roden returned to Mt. Carmel and at gunpoint forced Koresh and his followers to leave. After the death of Lois Roden, Koresh returned to Mt. Carmel with an armed group on November 3, 1987, seeking evidence that would discredit George Roden. A gunfight resulted that left Roden wounded. Koresh was charged with attempted murder. Later, the charge was dismissed, and Roden was imprisoned for violating restraining orders and for filing profanity-filled legal suits and motions. With George Roden's incarceration, and the late Lois Roden's blessings, David Koresh became the undisputed prophet of the Branch Davidians at Mt. Carmel.[43]

In explaining the history of the Davidians, David Bromley and Edward Silver identify two sociological typologies, the patronal clan and the prophetic movement organization. The following passage defines these terms:

> Patronal clans legitimate themselves as the most recent successors to an authentic spiritual lineage. The strongest temporal link thus is constructed between present and past as legitimation derives from tradition. Prophetic movements, by contrast, create legitimacy through stressing their role as creators of a new tradition. The temporal emphasis thus is on linking present and future.[44]

According to Bromley and Silver, both typologies inform the three eras of Davidian history: the periods of Houteff, Roden, and Koresh. During the first two eras the patronal clan model prevailed, although these periods began and ended with episodes of prophetic movement. In the Koresh era, on the other hand, the Davidians increasingly resembled a prophetic movement, at times still exhibiting the elements of a patronal clan.[45]

These typologies are effective tools for analyzing organizational histories, yet Bromley and Silver's conclusion that the Koresh era

---

[43]Bromley and Silver, "The Davidian Tradition," 54.
[44]Ibid., 44-45.
[45]Ibid.

was somehow variant is flawed. All three eras exhibited both typologies, moving back and forth between them in a cyclical manner. Because a BATF raid ended the Koresh era prematurely, his period appeared primarily prophetic. In fact, Koresh relied on the past tradition and his own prophetic revelations to legitimate his leadership. For example, he drew upon and enhanced tradition-al Seventh-day Adventist interpretations of the three angelic messages (Revelation 14:6-13) to affirm his role as prophet by contending that there were actually seven angels in the book of Revelation. The three messages/messengers espoused by Advent-ists were (1) Miller's proclamation of the "end times"; (2) Miller's decree that "Babylon" will fall; and (3) White's command to observe the seventh-day Sabbath.

> [Koresh argued that] the fourth [was] Victor Houteff, who in 1929 began to teach that there would be a literal, earthly Davidic Kingdom of God in Palestine. The fifth angel . . . he understood to be Ben Roden, who, around the year 1955, restored the observance of . . . biblical festival days. . . . The sixth messenger was recognized in Lois Roden, who in 1977 began to teach that the Holy Spirit was feminine. . . . Koresh saw himself as the seventh and last prophet. In accord with his 1985 revelation regarding Koresh/Cyrus as the final Christ figure, Koresh's own teachings drew upon those of his predecessors, from Miller through Lois Roden.[46]

---

[46]Tabor and Gallagher, *Why Waco?*, 49-50.

David Koresh and the Students of the Seven Seals[47]

David Koresh played a leading role in both the public's "cult" narrative and in the apocalyptic narrative of the Mt. Carmel community—a role largely predetermined by those narratives. The media described Koresh as the "Sinful Messiah";[48] government agents and much of the public thought of him as a self-aggrandizing "cult" leader. The Mt. Carmel community, "Students of the Seven Seals," believed he was the final Christ figure called to open the seven seals as outlined in the book of Revelation. Koresh was perceived quite differently in these two narratives.

The community living at Mt. Carmel accepted a worldview that many outsiders could not understand. Appreciating their reality required a thorough knowledge of the (King James Version) *Scofield Reference Bible* (especially the book of Revelation), the Seventh-day Adventist tradition, the Branch Davidian tradition, and the teachings of David Koresh. Conflict may sometimes be avoided by recognizing that one may not have a full understanding of reality and that one's worldview is negotiable and incomplete. In the Waco conflict, however, a number of communities clashed because they were unwilling or unable to see the limits of their own perspectives.

During the siege, Koresh composed two documents that explained the Davidian perspective. On March 1, the second day of the siege, the FBI offered Koresh national exposure for his

---

[47]Most of the community at Carmel did not call themselves Branch Davidians but "students of the seven seals." Originally, Victor Houteff named this group the Shepherd's Rod (in 1929) and then changed the name in 1942 to the Davidian Seventh-day Adventists to avoid the draft. The official name of this sect, as renamed by Ben Roden in 1962, is the General Association of Davidian Seventh-day Adventists. Unofficially, however, Roden referred to his community as Branch Davidians. Although Koresh did draw heavily upon the Seventh-day Adventist and Branch Davidian traditions, the focus of his community was to understand the mysteries of the seven seals. See Tabor and Gallagher, *Why Waco?*, 213.

[48]The day before the 28 February BATF raid of Mt. Carmel, the *Waco Tribune-Herald* began a week-long front-page series entitled "The Sinful Messiah," in which David Koresh is accused of bizarre sexual practices, child abuse, and paramilitary activities.

message in exchange for complete surrender. After much deliberation, Koresh released a fifty-eight-minute sermon on audiotape that
outlined his gospel to the world. Once the sermon had been aired,
the FBI expected everyone to exit the Mt. Carmel center; however,
Koresh informed them that God had told him to wait, and that he
would not surrender until God had told him to do so.[49]

The FBI agents were incensed by Koresh's change of plans and
believed from this point on that they could not trust him. Koresh
hinted at his reasons at the end of the March 2 sermon itself:

> We made an agreement, with the ATF agents, that if they
> would allow me to have national coverage with this tape: that I
> might give to the world . . . a small minute bit of the information
> that I have tried so hard to share with people; that I would do
> this, that all the people here at the facility . . . will give ourselves
> over to the world, give ourselves out to you. And this is what I
> promised. And this is what we're going to keep.
>
> Now remember, Revelation chapter 13 tells us, very clearly
> what our ideology should be toward that beast, and all the world
> that wonders after that beast. Who do they worship? Remember,
> before I said it to you. God said it. They worship the dragon. . . .
> But now in Spirit and in Truth, let's come up hither to where I
> come from. Let's believe in a God on the Throne now.[50]

Many criticized Koresh for lying. For Koresh, however, the government was the enemy he could never trust. According to his worldview, the U.S. government was an agent of the beast; Koresh, as a
follower of God, could never surrender to the beast unless God
instructed him to do so.

On April 14, the long wait was over when Koresh received his
"word from God." He sent the following letter to his lawyer, Dick
DeGuerin:

> I am presently being permitted to document, in structured form,
> the decoded messages of the Seven Seals. Upon completion of
> this task, I will be free of my "waiting period." I hope to finish

---

[49]Tabor and Gallagher, *Why Waco?*, 7.
[50]Koresh, *Sermon.*

this as soon as possible and to stand before man to answer any and all questions regarding my actions.

This written Revelation of the Seven Seals will not be sold, but is to be available to all who wish to know the Truth. The Four Angels of Revelation are here, now ready to punish foolish mankind; but, the writing of these Seals will cause the winds of God's wrath to be held back a little longer.

I have been praying so long for this opportunity; to put the Seals in written form. Speaking the Truth seems to have very little effect on man.

I was shown that as soon as I am given over into the hands of man, I will be made a spectacle of, and people will not be concerned about the truth of God, but just the bizarrity [sic] of me in the flesh.

I want the people of this generation to be saved. I am working night and day to complete my final work of the writing out of these Seals.

I thank my Father, He has finally granted me the chance to do this. It will bring New Light and hope for many and they will not have to deal with me the person.

I will demand the first manuscript of the Seals be given to you. Many scholars and religious leaders will wish to have copies for examination. I will keep a copy with me. As soon as I can see that people like Jim Tabor and Phil Arnold have a copy I will come out and then you can do your thing with this beast.[51]

No one will ever know whether Koresh would have fulfilled this promise to surrender. Five days later the FBI launched its assault upon the Mt. Carmel center, resulting in a fatal fire. A survivor of the fire, Ruth Riddle, escaped with a computer disk that contained an unfinished manuscript entitled "The Seven Seals of the Book of Revelation." She later revealed that on the weekend before the FBI attack, Koresh had dictated the entire contents of this manuscript, fulfilling his promise in the letter to his lawyer.

Both the sermon and the manuscript composed during the siege address the same audience, using many of the same biblical passages to present the same message: the mysteries of the seven seals from the book of Revelation. Koresh directed his message to

---

[51]Tabor and Gallagher, *Why Waco?*, 15-16.

Christians. Such people, he believed, took the life and sacrifice of Jesus Christ seriously, but may not have understood the importance of the book of Revelation. These documents were Koresh's principal means of sharing his insights about the "end times" with people he believed could come to share his worldview. For Koresh, his audience contained only two groups: those who immediately accepted his teachings and those who rejected them. In his world, the boundaries were fixed without much room for dialogue.

The sermon, taped on the third day of the siege, contains more of Koresh's own biblical commentary. The manuscript was written approximately forty-eight days later, when Koresh believed he had a specific mandate from God to reveal the mysteries of the seven seals. The sermon can be divided into an introduction, three content sections, and a conclusion. The unfinished manuscript contains a poetic preface, an introduction to the work as a whole, and chapter one, which considers the first seal.

Koresh follows Miller's hermeneutical principle, noted earlier, that "scripture must be its own expositor." For Koresh "every book of the Bible meets and ends in the book of Revelation."[52] He believes Revelation 1–3 refers to events that took place at the time of the prophetic book's composition; Revelation 4–22 describes the "end times." Thus, he interprets every biblical reference in light of his central text, Revelation 4–22 (King James Version).

Before Koresh can explain and justify his claim to be the final Christ figure, he must first challenge the dominant interpretation that the Lamb in Revelation represents the Christ of the first century: he must explain the difference between the Christ of the first century and the Christ of the "end times." Koresh's claim to be Christ led to much confusion throughout the fifty-one-day conflict.

Jim Wallis, in his article quoted above, contended that Koresh could not be Jesus Christ because he did not emulate the Jesus in the Gospels.[53] Koresh would have agreed with Wallis wholeheartedly. Koresh points out the similarities and the differences between himself and Jesus of Nazareth in both the sermon and the

---

[52]Koresh, *Seven Seals*, 197.
[53]Wallis, "Giving Religion a Bad Name," 50.

manuscript. In section one of the sermon, Koresh summarizes the life and death of Jesus, highlighting some of these similarities. Jesus of Nazareth was an uneducated man, born of a virgin, who performed many miracles and was recognized for his great knowledge of Scripture. As Koresh paraphrases him, Jesus claimed, "My doctrine is not mine, but his that sent me. If any man will do his will, he shall know of the doctrine, whether it be of God, or whether I speak of myself."[54] Nevertheless, Koresh continues, "the men of that generation would not believe in the man who through so many obvious evidences proved beyond shadows of doubt, that he was the Son of God,"[55] and the disciples of Christ "had to see (him) cruelly mocked, and beaten, and ridiculed, and rejected, and killed."[56]

In light of this description, the similarities between Koresh and Jesus of Nazareth are somewhat interesting. Koresh was born Vernon Howell on August 17, 1959, in Houston, Texas, to Bonnie Clark, an unwed fifteen-year-old mother. In 1981, he moved to the Mt. Carmel center, where he was hired as a carpenter and mechanic. The Branch Davidians at the time, including Lois Roden, marveled at how this seemingly uneducated man (a high school dropout) had such knowledge and command of the scriptures. David Koresh died at age 33 in a public event, at the hands of earthly authorities around the time of Passover, after his message, which he claimed was from God, had been rejected by the majority of the people who heard it. Even before Koresh's death, his followers believed he was the final Christ figure.[57]

While Koresh hinted at these similarities with the first-century Jesus, he forcefully explained the differences throughout the sermon and the manuscript. Koresh explained the role and characteristics of the final Christ figure and how this Christ is different from Jesus by using references in the Psalms, the prophets, the gospels, the Pauline letters, and 1 Peter to interpret Revelation 4–22. His explanation hinged on the meaning of *christos* as one

---

[54]Koresh, *Sermon.*
[55]Ibid. Koresh quotes here from the Gospel of John 7:16-17 (KJV).
[56]Ibid.
[57]Bromley and Silver, "The Davidian Tradition," 57.

anointed by God to fulfill a divine purpose—that "Christ" is not a proper name, but a title.[58] *Christos* is Greek for the Hebrew *mashiah*, or "anointed one," a title in ancient Israel that described divine appointment. Abraham, Isaac, and Jacob, as well as many of the Israelite priests and kings, are called "anointed" in the Hebrew Bible.

While visiting Israel in January 1985, Koresh (Vernon Howell at the time) received a revelation from God through the prophecy of Isaiah, known to his followers as the "Cyrus message." Isaiah 45:1 states that God anointed Cyrus (*Koresh* in Hebrew) to be the savior of Israel: "Thus saith the Lord to his anointed, to Cyrus, whose right hand I have holden, to subdue nations before him; and I will loose the loins of kings, to open before him the two-leaved gates; and the gates shall not be shut" (Isaiah 45:1 KJV). In 597 BCE Babylon had conquered Israel, deporting its people.[59] Cyrus of Persia defeated the ancient Babylonian empire in 539 BCE and allowed the deported Israelites to return to their own land.[60] According to Isaiah, this non-Israelite was chosen by the God of Israel to be a *mashiah* or *christos*. Vernon Howell, also a non-Israelite, felt himself called by God through this revelation to be a *christos* that would inaugurate the "end times." Therefore, he changed his name to "David Koresh" in 1990. David, the second King of Israel, had a "heart after God's own heart"; he led Israel during its most prosperous period, describing many of the "end time" mysteries in his book of Psalms.[61] Cyrus or *Koresh* saved Israel from the Babylonians, just as the Lamb conquers Babylon in the book of Revelation.[62] Koresh and his followers believed he was

---

[58]For discussion of the use of *christos* as both an appellative and a personal name in the New Testament, see Walter Bauer, *A Greek-English Lexicon of the New Testament and Early Christian Literature*, translated and adapted by William F. Arndt and F. Wilbur Gingrich; 2nd ed., revised and augmented by F. Wilbur Gingrich and Fredrick W. Danker from Walter Bauer's fifth edition, 1958 (Chicago: University of Chicago Press, 1979) s.v. Χριστός (886-87).

[59]J. Maxwell Miller and John H. Hayes, *A History of Ancient Israel and Judah* (Philadelphia: Westminster, 1986) 409-12.

[60]Ibid., 440-45.

[61]Koresh contended that "the key of David" referred to in Revelation 3:7 was a direct reference to the book of Psalms.

[62]Revelation 17–18.

Christ—not the Christ of the first century who preached nonviolence and was sacrificed, but a latter Christ in the legacies of David and Cyrus.

Two key texts for Koresh are Matthew 24 and Psalm 45. In his sermon, Koresh exegetes Matthew 24, Jesus' teaching concerning "end times" and the final Christ figure. Koresh's choice of text is rhetorically quite powerful because this passage also contains a warning against false prophets: "For many shall come in my name, saying, I am Christ; and shall deceive many" (Matthew 24:5 KJV). Koresh agrees with the interpretation that there shall be many false Christs. He gives special prominence to the following words of Jesus that describe the signs of the "end times":

> [15][Y]e, therefore, shall see the abomination of desolation, spoken of by Daniel the prophet. . . . [27][T]he lightning cometh out of the east, and shineth even unto the west; so shall also the Son of man be. [28]For wheresoever the carcase is, there will the eagles be gathered together. (Matthew 25:15, 27-28 KJV)

According to Koresh, Jesus taught that prophets like Daniel explained the events of these "end times." Koresh interprets "the lightning [that] cometh out of the east" and "the carcase" as references to himself. Further, he cites Isaiah 46:10-11a, the chapter after the reference to Cyrus:

> [10]Declaring the end from the beginning, and from ancient times the things that are not yet done, [the Lord] say[s], My counsel shall stand, and I will do all my pleasure: [11]Calling a ravenous bird from the east. . . . (Isaiah 46:10-11a KJV)

Koresh believed he was this "ravenous bird from the east." The bird in Isaiah 46 is the same as the lightning and the carcass in Matthew 24. As the final Christ figure, Koresh would come as a bird and a light from the east. Then in a battle associated with the sixth seal (Revelation 6:12-17), the Davidians in Palestine would join Israel to defend against an attack by an American-led, United Nations multilateral force from the north (the Babylon of the present). In this conflict Koresh would be killed, marred, and left to rot (Isaiah 52:14). From Revelation 6–16; Matthew 24:28; Daniel

11; Ezekiel 38; Zechariah 14; Psalm 89; and Isaiah 45–46, 52–53, Koresh developed this complex scenario of Armageddon.

However, Koresh did not believe these things would happen until he and the other Davidians had gathered the faithful children of God into a holy community, in anticipation of the final events. Part of these preparations are outlined in Psalm 45 and Revelation 19: the marriage of the Lamb/King, which both initiates the "end times" and anticipates the reign of God on earth. The greater part of Koresh's sermon and manuscript is an exegesis of Psalm 45. Koresh connects the king of Psalm 45 to the Lamb in Revelation in this way: the king who rode prosperously (Psalm 45:4) and shot arrows to kill his enemies (Psalm 45:5) is the same figure who rode on a white horse and carried a bow (Revelation 6:2) in reference to the first seal. Psalm 45 tells how this king, whose God wrote a Book and reigned forever, destroyed his enemies and took a spouse. In Revelation 17, the Lamb defeats Babylon; in chapter 19, he marries. The evidence that the Christ of Revelation conquers and marries, Koresh argues, cannot point to Jesus of Nazareth, but to another Christ who will come in the "end times."[63]

Koresh's "Cyrus message" justified his arms buildup and his marriage. It was a second, "New Light" revelation during the summer of 1989 that ultimately cost him his life and the lives of his children. Koresh's "New Light" revelation initiated the practice of celibacy among the Davidians, justified by biblical references such as Isaiah 2:19-22; Matthew 19:12; Luke 20:35; Galatians 3:28; 1 Corinthians 7:25-40; 2 Corinthians 5:17; and Revelation 14:4. This new revelation also disclosed that Koresh, the final Christ figure, must father twenty-four children who would become the twenty-four elders described in Revelation 4:1 and 5:8-10, Isaiah 53:10 and Psalm 45:16. From the teachings of Houteff, the Davidians believed they would hold leadership positions in an actual kingdom that God would establish in Palestine at the "end time." With this new revelation to the community, Koresh contended that his children would be the twenty-four elders in that divine kingdom.[64]

---

[63]James D. Tabor and J. Phillip Arnold, "Commentary on the Koresh Manuscript," in Tabor and Gallagher, *Why Waco?*, 206.

[64]Tabor and Gallagher, *Why Waco?*, 74-76.

On the day the FBI attacked the Mount Carmel center, U.S. Attorney General Janet Reno justified this action by claiming that the FBI had proof Koresh was abusing children. The original warrant against Koresh by the BATF mentions both the possession of illegal firearms and the physical and sexual abuse of children.[65] These sexual abuse charges are linked to the "New Light" revelation, pursuant to which Koresh fathered at least fifteen children with ten women; three of the mothers were girls under the age of eighteen (twelve, fourteen, and seventeen years old). This revelation and Koresh's subsequent sexual activity led some of the Davidians to leave the community and become prominent adversaries of Koresh.[66]

The faithful Davidians believed that Koresh was the one to reveal the mysteries of the seven seals, to gather the faithful servants of God, and to seal the 144,000. Koresh would participate in the events leading up to the Day of Judgment and father the twenty-four elders who were to rule with God. The Branch Davidians explicated the prophecies in Revelation by drawing together the new revelations of Koresh with their traditional teachings. This community inhabited a narrative universe that was significantly different from that of the enemies who confronted them during the fifty-one-day siege.

Why Take David Koresh and the Branch Davidians Seriously?

In U.S. society, where events are often remembered by video images, the burning of Mt. Carmel is the one image that has

---

[65]Child abuse was not under BATF's jurisdiction and the Children's Protective Services of Texas had terminated their investigation into the Mt. Carmel community the previous year (1992) because of lack of evidence. Thus many have called the attack an extreme measure.

[66]Christopher G. Ellison and John P. Bartkowski, "Babies Were Being Beaten: Exploring Child Abuse Allegations at Ranch Apocalypse," in Wright, *Armageddon*, 111-44. While I have sought in this essay to provide a view of Koresh and the Davidians that respects their religious beliefs, I do not support Koresh's alleged abusive actions. However, given the prejudice against this community, I contend that Koresh would not have had a fair hearing until the religious "cult" stereotypes surrounding the Davidians were dispelled.

defined this tragedy. During that fire, Mt. Carmel's flag was burned and by the time the fire had been extinguished someone had raised BATF's banner in its place.[67] Few people witnessed the hoisting of the BATF flag; yet in many ways this is the more telling and defining image. In a very real conflict, the winners were government agents and a society that saw Koresh and the Davidians as deviant religious fanatics. The defeated Davidians, instead, saw themselves as martyrs at the hands of the latter-day Babylon.[68]

In the last thirty years, there have been a number of clashes between government officials and marginalized groups. In 1978, a U.S. Representative and his party were killed by members of People's Temple in Jonestown, Guyana; 900 members of People's Temple later committed suicide.[69] In 1984, in Island Pond, Vermont, ninety Vermont state troopers raided the homes of the Community Church and took 112 children and their parents into custody because of child-abuse charges. The same day, a district court judge declared the raid unconstitutional.[70] In 1985, eleven members of MOVE, including four children, were killed in a Philadelphia fire after the local police firebombed an entire city block.[71]

Few people revel in tragedy, or the violation of civil freedoms. Yet most of us inhabit worlds that would not allow us to take a David Koresh, or any other "religious deviant," seriously. With the Mt. Carmel incident, we ignored the fact that the Davidians, the government agents, the media, and many of the religious commentators all drew from a common tradition. The conflicting parties were not radically divergent; they simply upheld different *interpretations* of the same American myth or emphasized different

---

[67]Dick J. Reavis, *The Ashes of Waco: An Investigation* (New York: Simon & Schuster, 1995) 277.

[68]Kelley, "Waco: A Massacre and Its Aftermath," 23, 34-35.

[69]Shupe and Bromley, *The New Vigilantes: Deprogrammers, Anti-Cultists, and the New Religions*, 210-11.

[70]Garret Keizer, *A Dresser of Sycamore Trees* (New York: HarperCollins, 1991) 110.

[71]Marc Galanter, *Cults: Faith, Healing, and Coercion* (New York: Oxford University Press, 1989) 124-28.

aspects of the same myth. Part of the main task of this essay then is difficult: to challenge both public and religious assumptions about religious communities that prevent effective dialogue with these groups, while at the same time understanding and respecting worldviews that seem actively to discourage such dialogue. In examining two varied critiques of the Branch Davidians, one from the media and the other by a religious scholar, I shall seek to construct a model that recognizes the traditions that both the Davidians and their critics share.

On February 27, 1993, just one day before the BATF raid, the *Waco Tribune-Herald* began a series on David Koresh and the Branch Davidians entitled "The Sinful Messiah." The day after the raid, the *Tribune-Herald* printed parts three through seven of this series and provided the public with its first analysis of Koresh and the Davidians. These sensationalized articles by Mark England and Darlene McCormick set the tone for much of the public discussion.

These articles emphasized scandalous allegations by ex-Davidians concerning child abuse and sexual misconduct by Koresh. Their description of the Davidians as a "bizarre spinoff of the Seventh-day Adventists . . . which mainline Adventists frankly consider to have rocketed off into orbit" separated this community from the larger religious American tradition. England and McCormick characterized this group as a "cult" whose leader "uses traditional mind-control techniques to entrap listeners," and whose "followers end up awash in Scripture, feeling [that] only [Koresh] has a true understanding of the Bible."[72] Such a characterization only fed the public's paranoia about marginalized religious communities, justifying the violence against them. Above all, the force of these articles trivialized the Davidians' religious beliefs by highlighting their leader's irreligious actions, underlining a purported lack of established religious tradition, and uncritically referencing the popular stereotype of "cult."

Craig Nessan, a professor of Contextual Theology at Wartburg Theological Seminary, responded to the Davidians' convictions and their misfortune out of his own religious faith. Nessan notes that

---

[72]Mark England and Darlene McCormick, "The Sinful Messiah," *Waco Tribune-Herald*, 27 February 1993, 28 February 1993, and 29 February 1993, sec. A.

while the Branch Davidians have a religious worldview that is "shared broadly in popular religious culture,"[73] the "religious ideas which contributed to [their] demise . . . are [founded] to a large degree on a tragic misreading of the Book of Revelation."[74] He describes the community that produced the book of Revelation as Christians who "anticipated God's dramatic intervention in history through natural disasters and the defeat of Rome. [This] would accompany the final return of Christ and the vindication of the Christian faithful."[75] However, Nessan argues that

> those [today] who employ the book to make magical predictions about current events and God's imminent intervention to end history not only distract energy away from addressing the world's problems but feed a religious mindset which is susceptible to the machinations of a David Koresh.[76]

Nessan's solution to this "problem" is to study the book of Revelation only "in its own original historical context."[77] He concludes:

> while we [Christians] are obliged to understand the origins and purpose [of this book] . . . the core of the Christian faith is centered in the gospel of Jesus Christ. The church [must] guard against those who manipulate the Bible according to their own self-serving and potentially destructive agenda.[78]

This analysis denies the Branch Davidians' freedom to imagine new worlds—to interpret the Bible, their scripture, in a way that supports their meaning-making and survival. Reflecting on his own religious experience, Nessan tells how he learned "about perseverance in the face of persecution, about resisting the idolatrous claims of governments, [and] about hope for a final resolution of

---

[73]Craig L. Nessan, "When Faith Turns Fatal: David Koresh and Tragic Misreadings of Revelation," *Currents in Theology and Mission* 22 (June 1995): 191.

[74]Ibid., 196.

[75]Ibid., 198.

[76]Ibid.

[77]Ibid.

[78]Ibid., 199.

history"[79] from the book of Revelation. In what way does the early church community differ from the Branch Davidians for Nessan or from the context of his own experience? The early church was persecuted by the Roman Empire and the Davidians by the U.S. government. Nessan legitimates the beliefs of the community that produced the book of Revelation, but regards the Branch Davidians' agenda as "self-serving and potentially destructive." In fact, all three agents construct a worldview that resists human authority perceived as oppressive.

Koresh and the Davidians were by some considered bizarre for possessing deep religious convictions, and thought by others to be misguided because of the beliefs they held. Both criticisms ignored the traditions that this community shared with the rest of American culture. We ourselves made them outsiders, then marked them as dangerous to the common good. Once they were perceived as a threat, the aggression released by the government was deemed to be justified.

Despite the prevailing opinion, the Branch Davidians were well integrated into the American myth. William Miller and David Koresh after him drew directly from the Puritan style of biblical interpretation. They believed the Bible not only explained history but revealed many things about the future, including when Christ would return. This sect of the Seventh-day Adventists had not sought to modernize its parent denomination, but to restore it to the past: to a time when people lived out their Bible, when prophets received revelations, explained the mysteries of God, and anticipated the return of Christ with great expectation. The Adventists, the Millerites, and even the Puritans before them sought such a community of faith. The Puritans came to North America in order to create a society that was faithful to God. "They came to prove that one could form a society so faithful, a church so cleansed, that even old England itself would be transformed by witnessing what determined believers had managed to achieve."[80] Like the Puritans, the Davidians believed they had been

---

[79]Ibid., 198.

[80]Edwin Scott Gaustad, *A Religious History of America*, new rev. ed. (San Francisco: HarperSanFrancisco, 1990) 56.

selected by God to purify their church and to be an example of faithfulness to the world.

The themes and content of the two public documents Koresh released during the siege relate to the American myth. By interpreting the Bible typologically, Koresh and his community believed Babylon was the U.S. government, not merely a kingdom that conquered the Israelites centuries ago. They were the "firstfruits," God's faithful as described in Revelation 14:4, who would stand with God during the final battle against Babylon. Then Babylon "shall make war with the Lamb, and the Lamb shall overcome them; for he is Lord of lords, and King of kings: and they that are with him are called, and chosen, and faithful" (Revelation 17:14 KJV).

Koresh, in these documents, believed he was fulfilling the mission God had chosen for him: "I'm involved in a very serious thing right now . . . but I am really concerned about the lives of my brethren here, and also would be concerned even [more], about the lives of all those in this world."[81] Even while involved in a standoff with the federal government, Koresh seemed to be burdened for everyone in the world who was not a member of his community. The concluding paragraph of the sermon reveals Koresh's target audience:

> Revelation chapter 13 tells us, very clearly what our ideology should be toward that beast. . . . Who do they worship? . . . They worship the dragon. . . . But now in Spirit and in Truth, let's come up hither to where I come from . . . let's get into unity with one God, one Truth, one Lamb, one Spirit—and let's receive the reward of righteousness.[82]

Koresh directs his message toward "us"—persons who are in the Spirit, whom God has selected as "firstfruits." "They" are the enemy—those who worship the beast, subjects of the kingdom of Babylon. The final statement is a reference to Revelation 22:11-12, where the reward is a heavenly kingdom free of Babylon's

---

[81]Koresh, *Sermon* [n.p.].
[82]Ibid.

oppression. The Davidians, like their Puritan ancestors, sought to establish just such a community.

The critics cited child abuse, sexual misconduct, and the stock-piling of weapons as the primary reasons to condemn David Koresh and the Branch Davidians—allegations which separated them from the public, including other Christians.[83] For the Davidians, however, such a separation was assumed to be theologically necessary. Here, the sources of their biblical-interpretative framework and of their theology provide the key for understanding the Davidians within the broader U.S. society. This community showed its allegiance to God by withdrawing from society and living together in a social structure that reflected this separation. Members of the Davidians, except Koresh and his spiritual wives, became celibate in 1990 after the "New Light" revelation. In 1991, Koresh began gathering weapons and supplies to prepare for the Apocalypse. As Christians, the Davidians believed themselves called to these steps.

John Collins, along with many scholars, argues that "apocalypticism . . . was surely one crucial ingredient in the formation of the new religion [Christianity]."[84] The apocalyptic and gnostic movements, spreading among Jewish and Christian communities in the first and second centuries CE, were seminal to the development of Christianity. An apocalyptic worldview that perceives "the radical dichotomy between the present age and the age to come, and . . . despair(s) of anything good arising out of the present,"[85] is clearly a worldview that challenges earthly authority.

Many Christians and other religious commentators contend that while apocalypticism is an important aspect of Christian history, it should not constitute the worldview of modern Christians. This claim ignores a vital, if not the central, teaching of

---

[83]See England and McCormick. For a detailed analysis of how government agents and news media shaped public opinion of the Davidians, see Anson Shupe and Jeffrey K. Hadden, "Cops, News Copy, and Public Opinion: Legitimacy and the Social Construction of Evil in Waco," in Wright, *Armageddon*, 177-202.

[84]John J. Collins, *The Apocalyptic Imagination: An Introduction to the Jewish Matrix of Christianity* (New York: Crossroad, 1984) 206-207.

[85]Christopher Rowland, *The Open Heaven: A Study of Apocalyptic in Judaism and Early Christianity* (London: SPCK, 1982) 25.

Christianity itself. Tim Parks, in a short story that explains his own experiences with religion, describes the Christian tradition:

> Called out of this world, the Christian is given the mission of getting the world straight before it is too late, not of loving it for what it is. Thus all Christian sanctity tends toward apocalypse, until, frustrated, it settles for immolation. Even for those of us who do not believe (myself now among them), this state of mind is not incomprehensible. We have had our passions and epiphanies, the intensities we have tried to cling to. We can recognize the saint's peculiar heroism, the seduction of his folly: to hold a faith rigid across the decades, and then, when weary, to find some way of dying for it."[86]

The consequences of such living may lead to immolation and a number of other actions that do not seem congruent with the modern American-Christian way of life. However, this assumption overlooks the vibrant nature of religious traditions:

> In the dynamic mutations of doctrine through generations of religious leadership, we may perceive an age-old pattern governing the formation of apocalyptic communities. It is a dialectical process of community building and critique, in which eschatological myth inspires a group to withdraw from society or from a church in anticipation of a coming Judgment, only to find that the preaching of imminent doom leads unexpectedly to prosperity and formal establishment of yet another church, which may in turn spawn its own dissident prophets, and so on ad infinitum.[87]

The Davidians' active participation in the "dialectical process" with the larger mythical and religious traditions in the United States led them to their apocalypticism.

Despite popular opinion, I contend that the Branch Davidians sought to live out the very myths and traditions that U.S. society safeguards. When a government expends the level of resources and energy that the U.S. government did on the Waco crisis, one

---

[86]Tim Parks, "Fidelity: Midlife crisis and the sanctity of St. Timothy," *The New Yorker* (23 and 30 December 1996): 59.

[87]O'Leary, *Arguing the Apocalypse*, 226.

wonders what was really at stake. Given the results of the siege, the FBI's primary concern was probably not the welfare of those inside Mt. Carmel. Were the government agents and their many supporters frightened to encounter people who lived out the American myth too intensely? Were many of the Davidians' fellow Christians appalled to see where fervent faith could lead? Do we really want these myths to be realized? Instead of condemning communities like the Davidians, we may need to challenge the myths and traditions we hold so dear. Martyrdom, self-sacrifice, and immolation are not merely the tenets of "bizarre" religious communities, but significant parts of our long Western Christian and U.S. Christian heritage.

Heaven's Gate
Religious Outworldliness American Style

Rosamond Rodman

Introduction

On Wednesday afternoon, 26 March 1997, sheriff's deputies responded to a call in the wealthy San Diego suburb of Rancho Santa Fe. Inside the house to which they had been summoned, the deputies found thirty-nine bodies, all similarly clad and shrouded in purple cloth, dead from apparent suicide. It took several days for the story of "Heaven's Gate" to emerge. Television anchors, radio producers, and newspaper reporters turned to "religious experts"—mainly clergy—to piece together some explanations concerning the largest ever mass suicide in North America. Why had they done it? What to make of Heaven's Gate's strange, syncretic brew of Bible, UFOs, and New Age spirituality?

In seminaries, divinity schools, and graduate programs in religious and theological studies, students are taught to read carefully and critically the texts that are called scriptures or the Bible. They are encouraged to learn the ancient languages. They are pressed to acknowledge the social, historical, and religious situations from which biblical texts emerged, and they are required to produce incisive exegesis papers. But the differences between what religious and theological students learn and what Heaven's Gate represents seems an almost unbridgeable gap. How does such academic training help confront *contemporary* situations in which the Bible is of paramount importance, as was the case with Heaven's Gate? How can students of the Bible mobilize their hard-earned skills to

The Heaven's Gate "home page" at mirror site www.heavensgatetoo.com.

approach the Bible as a complex cultural force instead of as a set of antiquarian texts available only to a few highly trained exegetes? For example, Heaven's Gate referred to the Bible in particular ways, preferred certain translations to others, and in many ways defined itself as a biblical formation. Yet biblical scholarship, on the whole, does not address and analyze such a contemporary phenomenon, nor discuss how interpretive communities, such as Heaven's Gate, might be relevant to the field.

Charles Mabee's book, *Reading Sacred Texts through American Eyes: Biblical Interpretation as Cultural Critique,* is useful in pointing to the ways in which biblical interpretation could be applied to the Heaven's Gate phenomenon.[1] Mabee articulates the need to situate readings of the Bible within American culture, an approach he calls "American biblical hermeneutics."[2] Mabee's approach focuses analysis not on the Bible alone (or any specific biblical text), but on interpretive communities and their interactions with the Bible. Mabee's book calls for "a new way of integrating sacred text and public culture that retains the critical spirit of each."[3] This approach challenges scholars and religious leaders to speak to the gaps and exchanges between the academic study of scripture and popular contemporary American interpreters and practitioners of scripture. This necessarily involves a self-critical awareness of "that part of the American experience that lies hidden beneath the surface of everyday existence but is presupposed by it."[4] For the scholar no less than the contemporary American religious (of whatever denomination or cult), the Bible is central to American identity.

> A product of other cultures, it [the Bible] is yet the bearer of our own deepest societal aspirations. . . . The social and political events of our time give witness to the enormous appeal of underwriting the status quo through reference to commonly held ideas of what the Bible says, but this appeal shows remarkably little hermeneutical sophistication and wrestling with actual biblical texts. A public reading of the Bible addresses this problem by incorporating ongoing ecclesiastical and academic interpretive

---

[1]Charles Mabee, *Reading Sacred Texts through American Eyes: Biblical Interpretation as Cultural Critique,* StABH 7 (Macon GA: Mercer University Press, 1991).
[2]Ibid. See especially the introduction, and passim.
[3]Ibid., 4.
[4]Ibid., 21.

communities while moving beyond them to issues of common cultural concern.[5]

Mabee's model of a "public reading of the Bible" offers a helpful approach to an interpretation of the Heaven's Gate phenomenon. The media and the religious experts they engaged offered numerous explanations for the "extremism" displayed by Heaven's Gate. Many depictions focused on the tragic end to which the group had come, but otherwise portrayed a somewhat cartoonish portrait of the group's religious identity. The academic community, on the other hand, largely ignored it. American biblical hermeneutics offers another option: Heaven's Gate is one point on a trajectory of a complicated American religious history. It was not unique. The limits of this essay prevent a more thorough historical survey, but a brief look into the rhetoric of an early "New World" settler provides a remarkable phenomenological analogue to and historical perspective upon Heaven's Gate.

"We Shall Be as a City Upon a Hill . . . "

John Winthrop, who was to become the first governor of Massachusetts Bay Colony in 1630, delivered a homiletic address aboard the flagship *Arbella* as he and a small band of Puritans were crossing the Atlantic to found a "New World." Winthrop's address is liberally peppered with references to biblical passages. His message claimed that the group's voyage was a response to what God called on them as true Christians to do, and that the success of their difficult passage across the Atlantic ocean depended upon their "strict performance of the Articles" contained in their covenant with God.

In order to enact God's commandments as set forth in the Bible, Winthrop and the other Europeans had to find a new land, a "New World" in which "ourselves and [our] posterity may be the better preserved from the Common corrupcions of this evill world, to serve the Lord and work out our Salvacion under the power and purity of his holy Ordinances."[6] The company per-

---

[5]Ibid., 5.
[6]John Winthrop's sermon, "A Modell of Christian Charity" is available in vari-

ceived itself to be leaving behind a world which was hopelessly corrupt. The Old World could not contain the vision of purity and grace that Winthrop called "the Gospell lawe."[7] In the Old World, the "lawe of nature" prevailed.[8] So Winthrop and others had to found a "New England," a place in which "the Gospell lawe" would rule. The New World would provide "much more of His wisdome power goodnes and truthe than formerly wee have beene acquainted with."[9] The New World was, of course, more than a place. Their "outwardly" orientation actually described a way of being in the world, regardless of geographical situation.[10] Winthrop warned his fellow voyagers about the importance of keeping this outworldly rigorous stance. He warned that were the group to embrace the world, its carnal and material ways, then "The Lord will surely breake out in wrath against us . . . and make us knowe the price of the breache of such a Covenant."[11]

Winthrop's company endured a difficult and not altogether routine voyage to realize its mission. Leaving behind families, homes, and respectable careers (Winthrop was himself a lawyer), this small band of religious visionaries left behind a familiar world to found one based on their religious calling. They relied on the relatively new technology of seaworthy boats as the means for their mission.[12] The availability of Atlantic crossing was itself an

---

ous publications. In this essay I use the text in Giles Gunn's sourcebook, *New World Metaphysics* (New York: Oxford University Press, 1987) 50-54. An authentic copy of the document also may be found on the internet at http://boserup.qal.berkeley.edu/~gene/145/documents/wintrhop.modell.htm.

[7]Ibid., 52.

[8]Ibid.

[9]Ibid., 53.

[10]Outworldliness and the emergence of the outworldly individual have received excellent comparative and historical treatment by Louis Dumont in his *Essays on Individualism*. Dumont traces the problem facing the Christian individual, at first a stranger to the world, but then through time, more and more involved in it. Dumont examines this development by way of Max Weber's "inworldly" and "outworldly" ascetical stances. Louis Dumont, *Essays on Individualism: Modern Ideology in Anthropological Perspective* (Chicago: University of Chicago Press, 1986).

[11]Gunn, *New World Metaphysics*, 53

[12]On board the *Talbot*, which had set off in the wake of the *Arbella*, fourteen passengers died of illness and/or malnourishment by the time it arrived on new world shores. John Adair, *Founding Fathers. The Puritans in England and America*

affirmation of their vision, especially when Atlantic crossings were no easy task. Their break with the Old World was an enormous risk. Wilderness, harsh winters, and physical travail awaited them. The lack of personal comfort or even personal security seemed to pose no threat to the group. Winthrop's homily reflects the promise the New World holds. "[W]ee shall be as a Citty upon a Hill. . . . "[13] In itself, the *Arbella*'s successful passage would serve either to affirm or deny the integrity of their mission. "Now if the Lord shall please to heare us, and bring us in peace to the place wee desire, then hath hee ratified this Covnenant and sealed our Commission. . . . "[14] Thus, the *Arbella*'s successful journey relied on the integrity of their strictly following what the Bible says—"Now the onely way to avoyde this shipwracke, and to provide for our posterity, is to followe the counsell of Micah. . . . "[15] Leaving the Isle of Wight on the 29th of March, the *Arbella* reached the New World shores on June 8, 1630. The ideology of these first religious seekers remains etched in the landscape of American religious thought.

Heaven's Gate appears as one point on a historical trajectory that began with Winthrop and Europeans like him—adventurous and intense, hypercritical and in some respects alienated from and marginalized in their world. Winthrop's refusal to participate in the "old world," his embarking for new world shores, and his identification of the Bible as map for his outworldly journey, find remarkable analogues in Heaven's Gate's expressions.

The Evolutionary Level beyond Human

Heaven's Gate began in the early 1970s, the outgrowth of a partnership between voice professor Marshall Herff Applewhite (1931–1997) and registered nurse Bonnie Lu Trousdale Nettles (d. 1985).[16] "The Two," as they then called themselves, began attract-

---

(London: J. M. Dent & Sons, 1982) 11.

[13]Gunn, *New World Metaphysics*, 53.

[14]Ibid.

[15]Ibid.

[16]Barry Bearak, "Eyes on Glory: Pied Pipers of Heaven's Gate," *New York Times*, 28 April 1997, A1, B8-10.

ing students and disciples to join them. To do so required a serious commitment to leave one's job, home, and family, and to forego all material possessions and past relations.[17] All of those who joined were required to eschew their given names and adopt a new, typically one-word name. Nettles and Applewhite themselves took names like "Guinea" and "Pig" (a wry reference to their role in a "cosmic experiment"), "Bo" and "Peep," and finally "Ti" and "Do." The renaming process was an important part of deconstructing their former identities and reconstructing new ones. They began to refer to themselves collectively as the "Total Overcomers," in reference to their intention to overcome their earthly existence. Eventually, they changed the name of the group to "Heaven's Gate."

As the years went by, more people joined. Members took occasional odd jobs for money to supplement dwindling savings and trust funds. They traveled fairly constantly, although there were periods of time when the group would stay in one location for a year or so. They held teach-ins and public meetings to spread their message. Their recruitment techniques were almost bashful, consisting mostly of public talks in homes and church basements, which they advertised by putting up signs only a day or sometimes mere hours before the meetings were to take place.[18]

From the mid-1980s through the time of their "departure," Heaven's Gate communicated more and more by computers, using computer technology—modems, the World Wide Web, and the Internet—to spread its message and attract followers. The group created a website that contained transcriptions of videotaped question-and-answer sessions with "Do," autobiographical statements by members of the group, texts from posters and informational statements, and the text of an entire book compiled by "students" and entitled *How and When "Heaven's Gate" May Be Entered.*[19] The

---

[17]For a nice synopsis of the early history of the group, see Robert Balch's "Waiting for the Ships: Disillusionment and the Revitalization of Faith in Bo and Peep's UFO Cult," in *The Gods Have Landed: New Religions from Other Worlds*, ed. James R. Lewis (Albany: State University of New York Press, 1995).

[18]Frank Bruni, "Odyssey of Regimentation Carried Cult over Decades, *New York Times*, 29 April 1997.

[19]This first version of this anthology was self-published in 1996. As instructed

artwork on the site features friendly looking extraterrestrials, the swirling reddish clouds of galaxy formations, and shining celestial bodies against a backdrop of black (see the black-and-white reproduction of the homepage logo on 158, above).[20]

The single most common reference on the Heaven's Gate website is to the "Evolutionary Level above Human" (whence of course the acronym TELAH). The community referred to this alternately as the "Kingdom of Heaven," "our Father's Kingdom," or simply, "the Level above Human." Heaven's Gate members saw themselves constantly on the verge of departing for the Evolutionary Level above Human. In the meantime, their task on earth was to cultivate themselves and others to be ready to go to the Level above Human. They did this through renunciation of their bodies, and of the "world," and through their evangelization efforts.

The members of the group considered their human bodies to be mere "vehicles," "containers," or "receptables" for the soul.[21] Some of the men, including "Do" himself, seemed to have opted for surgical castration. Cooking, eating, bathing, and sleeping were seen as mere maintenance functions, practiced only to keep "the vehicle" of the human body going. The group members all dressed alike, wearing simple dark pants, a plain, usually white shirt, and

---

by the group prior to their "departure," the Telah Foundation published the third and final version of the book in March 1998. This version was completed just days before the "departure," with the full title as follows: *How and When "Heaven's Gate" (the Door to the Physical Kingdom Level above Human) May Be Entered: An Anthology of Our Materials* (Mill Spring NC: Blue Water Publishing/Wild Flower Press, March 1998) about 320 pages. (A reprint by Right to Know Enterprises, Denver, in 1997 was—according to Telah Foundation—unauthorized, "not completely accurate," and has been withdrawn.)

[20]The original Heaven's Gate website (www.heavensgate.com) was not accessible during the writing of this essay. I relied upon "mirror sites," of which there are about a dozen to be found by searching the internet for "Heaven's Gate." Currently, the only websites authorized by the Telah Foundation, holder of the copyright to the original website, are www.heavensgatetoo.com and www.levelabovehuman.org. Both of these sites were active and accessible as of May 1999. The Telah Foundation reports that the original website will be brought back up soon in its original format. Prior to granting permission for the use of the website materials, the Telah Foundation was provided a copy of this essay. I would like to acknowledge their helpful suggestions and corrections.

[21]See "Do's Intro: Purpose—Belief. What Our Purpose Is—The Simple Bottom Line" at http://www.heavensgatetoo.com/intro.htm.

running shoes. Women and men kept their hair closely cropped. The group seemed to have believed that bodies are merely borrowed. The soul wears a physical body in order to carry out particular tasks for the Evolutionary Level above Human. Jesus himself is thought to have been a member of the Evolutionary Level above Human who was instructed by his Father to move into a human body.[22] This member's sole task was to "offer the way leading to membership into the Kingdom of Heaven."[23] When it was time, the representative from the Kingdom of Heaven received instructions to leave behind his "vehicle" and reascend to the Level Above. "Do," referring to himself as an "undercover Jesus," explained that he and the group were in precisely the same situation that Jesus and his followers were in 2,000 years ago.

> [W]e were identified as a small, radical cult, just as we were 2,000 years ago. And as was the case 2,000 years ago, these prospective members left their families and relationships to follow or be a student. . . . I will again be hated for my "blasphemy" (of who I say I am) and hated by those families and others that are affected by all who aspire to leave with us, because this mission requires that they forsake all ties and binds to this world. . . . [24]

Like the seventeenth-century Europeans aboard the *Arbella*, Heaven's Gate's motivation was also to leave home—the world. They too cut social, professional, and family relations. Although some would argue that the Europeans were not as histrionic in tone (or fate) as the Heaven's Gate group, they made a radical break from all that they knew in order to realize their "special providence." In the age of the *Concord's* three-hour Atlantic crossing, it is easy to forget or minimize the magnitude of their voyage. The similarity between Heaven's Gate and John Winthrop's rhetoric must certainly not be pushed too far. They emerge from entirely different historical moments and cultural contexts.

---

[22]This event was understood in terms of adoptionist theology via a reading of Jesus' baptism by John as recorded in Luke 3:22.

[23]See www.heavensgatetoo.com.

[24]"Undercover 'Jesus' Surfaces before Departure" (from Do's "exit statement"), in *How and When "Heaven's Gate" May Be Entered*, 1.3-1.4, and at http://heavensgatetoo.com/book/1-2.htm.

But reading Heaven's Gate as one point on an ideological trajectory, which also includes some seventeenth-century European religious persons who sought a new world, provides greater perspective not only on Heaven's Gate, but also on American religious ideology in general.

Both groups saw this world as corrupt and evil. Their religious vision could not be realized in "the world." Both groups had to leave the world. For Heaven's Gate, the world was such that all institutions, including religious ones, worked for the advancement of evil forces. Lucifer captained these forces, and he was the personification of all the evil at work in the world. Heaven's Gate spoke of "this world" only in pejorative terms, captive to "Luciferian forces." This world entraps the true seeker. The world of "human-mammalian characteristics" prevents even the most pious from realizing their captivity to the "Luciferian" or "lower forces."

> Many segments of society, especially segments of the religious, think that they are *not* "of the world," but rather that their "conversion" experience finds them *outside of* worldliness." . . . Unless you are currently an active student or are attempting to become a student of the present Representative from the Kingdom of Heaven—you *ARE STILL* "of the world," having done *no significant* separation from worldliness, and you are still serving the *opposition* to the Kingdom of Heaven.[25]

Strongly dualistic, Heaven's Gate saw that relinquishing connections to the world was its passage into the Evolutionary Level above Human. Making specific reference to worldliness, the group defined itself as belonging *not* to this world.

The second most characteristic feature of the Heaven's Gate website is its numerous references to the Bible. The website repeatedly refers to Do's analogy to Jesus, and to the Kingdom of Heaven. Even the science fiction references (mostly to extraterrestrials and UFOs) are situated within a biblical paradigm. "We will rendezvous in the 'clouds' (a giant mothership) for our briefing

---

[25]"Do's Intro," in *How and When "Heaven's Gate" May Be Entered*, v, and at www.heavensgatetoo.com.

and journey to the Kingdom of the Literal Heavens"[26] (cf. 1 Thess 4:17). "If you can get your name in our 'book,' on our spacecraft's computer . . . then you will go with us"[27] (cf. Rev 20:15).

Heaven's Gate preferred a "red-letter" Bible, and was partial especially to the *Amplified Bible*.[28] For the most part, the group seemed to think that the Bible as a written document had been tainted by the world, mistranslated and misunderstood, "corrupted by . . . councils of so-called scholars." It was deemed "miraculous" that the "formula for transition from the human kingdom to the Level above Human has been preserved in Jesus' requirements for discipleship."[29] For this reason, they preferred the clarity that the *Amplified Bible* afforded. For all of its problems, the Bible remained the only historical record of a time when the Evolutionary Level above Human had sent a representative (Jesus). The Bible still offered the "only historical record . . . of when the Next Level was relating to man."[30] The group's on-line book includes an appendix consisting solely of quotations from the Bible that were determined to be relatively accurate teachings. This appendix features quotations of Jesus' sayings. These quotations are grouped under headings such as "Breaking Away from the World," "Recognizing, Believing, and Following the Representative from the Kingdom of Heaven," and "Soul vs. Flesh Body."[31]

---

[26]See " '95 Statement by an E.T. Presently Incarnate (slightly edited) January 1997," *How and When "Heaven's Gate" May Be Entered*, 1.7, and at www.heavens-gatetoo.com/95upd96.htm.

[27]See "UFO Cult Resurfaces with Final Offer." This statement appeared originally in a paid advertisement in *USA Today* (27 May 1993); it was later added to the HG website, now at http://www.heavensgatetoo.com/book/5-2.htm, then printed in *How and When "Heaven's Gate" May Be Entered*, 5.3.

[28]*The Amplified Bible: Containing the Amplified Old Testament and the Amplified New Testament* (Grand Rapids MI: Zondervan, ©1965). The introduction to appendix B (see n. 29, below) in *How and When "Heaven's Gate" May Be Entered* explains: "We chose to use *The Amplified Bible* (translation), with a few exceptions, for its clarity." This preference statement is then "amplified" with several quotations from the preface and introduction to the *Amplified Bible*.

[29]See the introduction to "Bible Quotes Primarily from Previous Representatives to Earth from the Evolutionary Level above Human," appendix B to *How and When "Heaven's Gate" May Be Entered*, accessible at http://www.heavensgate-too.com/book/b-1.htm.

[30]Ibid.

[31]Ibid.

The appendix also reveals Heaven's Gate's preference for the Gospel of John. Quotations from this gospel occur fully twice as often as quotations from any other part of the Bible. This is not surprising. The Jesus of the Gospel of John is a descending and ascending revealer who speaks of the "world" in negative terms. Like this Jesus, "Do" considered himself a revealer who testified to the corruption of this world, and would lead followers to the Level Above. The Gospel of John speaks of "a man from above" who came to earth to teach those who were willing to overcome their human existence the way to the Level Beyond Human (cf. John 1:14ff.; 3:13-21; 6:32-51). This portrayal was certainly not lost on Heaven's Gate.

Both Winthrop's rhetoric and the Heaven's Gate website literature articulate "outworldly" mission as one that had already, in some sense, been mapped out and was revealed in the Bible. The centrality of the Bible in both sets of rhetoric reveals another case for comparison. As a force in American cultural identity formation, the Bible holds center stage. American cultural-religious identity can hardly be considered without it (which is not the same thing as saying that religious identity in America cannot be expressed without it). The Bible in America is what Martin Marty calls "an icon."[32] It is a totem, representing a fundamental sense of identity.

The ultimate affirmation of Heaven's Gate came when the Hale-Bopp comet entered the earth's atmosphere. The Hale-Bopp comet was the sign for which the group had long been waiting— the Evolutionary Level was finally sending a spacecraft to Earth to pick them up. The spacecraft/comet signaled Heaven's Gate's place on a timeline that began 2,000 years ago when Jesus put on human flesh. Now, with the arrival of the spaceship, Heaven's Gate members would discard their bodies. They neatly packed overnight bags with clothes, spiral notebooks, lip balm, and pocket change. They mixed lethal doses of phenobarbital into applesauce and laid upon their beds with plastic bags secured over their heads in case the drug did not work. In this way, a group of thirty-nine people "departed" during the zenith of the Hale-Bopp comet, an

---

[32]See Martin E. Marty, *Religion and Republic: The American Circumstance* (Boston: Beacon Press, 1987) 140-65.

event that constituted the largest mass suicide in North American history.

As the American public reached for explanations, religious experts reached for answers. Most of them, when questioned by the media, offered explanations about the dangers of cults or charismatic leaders. It was more difficult to imagine Heaven's Gate as embodying an ideal upon which "America" as an "outworldly" religious formation was founded. Yet the group should be situated within a longstanding tradition of American religious outworldliness. As one moment in a trajectory that reaches back to Winthrop's articulation of "A Modell of Christian Charity," Heaven's Gate rhetoric is not very different in type from that of the Puritan's New World that, along with other trajectories, defined America.

Conclusions

Heaven's Gate offers the student of religion an opportunity to experiment with new ways to engage scripture, and new ways of thinking about how scripture functions in interpretive communities. Consider two approaches that might join Mabee's "American biblical hermeneutics" as a type of scholarship in connection with the Bible.

One approach might study interpretive communities and the scriptural texts they engage. This approach would refocus exegetical studies—away from ancient texts, toward contemporary communities. For example, Heaven's Gate identified most strongly with the Gospel of John. Learning about Heaven's Gate, its readings of the Bible, and its preference for the Gospel of John brings Wayne Meek's famous essay, "The Man from Heaven in Johannine Sectarianism,"[33] to mind. Meek's careful word study, his awareness of literary structure and rhetorical devices, and his application of sociological models show how rigorous academic biblical scholarship can be. His essay models what careful attention to language patterns can yield. Yet revisiting Meek's essay in light of the Heaven's Gate phenomenon means nuancing one of his concluding

---

[33]Wayne A. Meeks "*The* Man from Heaven in Johannine Sectarianism," *Journal of Biblical Literature* 91 (1972): 44-72.

statements: "Faith in Jesus, in the fourth Gospel, means a removal from 'the world,' because it means transfer to a community that has totalistic and exclusive claims."[34] Meek's essay can help illuminate and account for a late modern American religious group, which modeled itself on a particular reading of the Johannine community.

But there may also be illumination of the Johannine and related communities in the ancient world in the critical reading of late modern formations such as Heaven's Gate. Modern and contemporary "outworldly" readings, constructions, and performative acts—obviously more accessible, perhaps more complex—may shed light on the complexity of socioreligious formations of the ancient world. Such an approach situates interpretive communities and their totemic texts as complexes of identity making. In this way, students of religion could examine not only religious texts, but also the religious experiences that gives rise to such texts.

Another approach calls for a typological reading. This approach spans time and culture as well, but with an effort to draw parallels against a larger historical backdrop. For example, the parallels between Heaven's Gate and gnosticism were mentioned during the time of the feverish press coverage of Heaven's Gate.[35] Their asceticisms and their harshly defined polarities between the human level and the Evolutionary Level above Human brought ancient gnosticism's infamous dualism to mind. There is, for example, a striking similarity between Heaven's Gate's anthropology and that of the ancient gnostic text *The Tripartite Tractate*. According to Heaven's Gate's understanding of the origins of humankind, all humans fall into three categories:

(i) Humans without deposits—those who are simply "plants" . . . ,

(ii) those with deposits/souls who are receiving nourishment from the present Rep[resentative](s) toward metamorphic completion, and

---

[34]Ibid., 71.

[35]See, e.g., Kenneth Woodward, "Christ and Comets," *Newsweek* (7 April 1997): 40-43; and Mark Dery, "The Cult of the Mind," *New York Times Magazine* (28 September 1997): 94-96.

(iii) those with deposits/souls who are not in a classroom nor in a direct relationship with the Representative(s) from the Level Beyond Human. . . . [36]

These categories mirror *The Tripartite Tractate's* three divisions of humankind:

Mankind came to be in three essential types, the spiritual, the psychic and the material, conforming to the triple disposition of the Logos, from which were brought forth the material ones and psychic ones and the spiritual ones. Each of the three essential types is known by its fruit. And they were not known at first, but only at the coming of the Savior, who shone upon the saints and revealed what each was.[37]

Notwithstanding the lack of a unified definition, interpreters have tried to explain complex historical phenomena by reference to "gnosticism."[38] For example, Giovanni Filoramo finds in "gnosticism" a "pertinent guide to those processes of social restructuring, of ideological transformation, of change in religious sentiment that characterizes *our age also.*"[39] But perhaps the best example, for the purposes of this essay, is Harold Bloom's book *The American Religion* in which Bloom develops a fascinating connection between

---

[36]From " '95 Statement by an E.T. Presently Incarnate (slightly edited) January 1997," in *How and When "Heaven's Gate" May Be Entered*, 1.9, and at www.heavensgatetoo.com/95upd96.htm.

[37]*The Tripartite Tractate*, trans. Harold Attridge and Dieter Mueller, in *The Nag Hammadi Library*, rev. ed., ed. James Robinson (San Francisco: Harper & Row, 1988) §118, p. 94.

[38]See Hans Jonas, *The Gnostic Religion*, 2nd rev. ed. (Boston: Beacon Press, 1958) 32-46; Kurt Rudolph, "Gnosis and Gnosticism—The Problems of Their Definition and Their Relationship to the Writings of the New Testament," in *The New Testament and Gnosis: Essays in Honour of Robert McLachlan Wilson*, ed. A. H. B. Logan and A. J. M. Wedderburn (Edinburgh: T. & T. Clark, 1983) 21-37; Ioan Coulianu, "The Gnostic Revenge: Gnosticism and Romantic Literature," in *Religionstheorie und Politische Theologie*, Band 2. *Gnosis und Politik*, ed. Jacob Taubes (Munich, Padderborn, Vienna, and Zurich: Wilhelm Fink/Ferdinand Schoeningh, 1984) 290-91; Elaine Pagels, *The Gnostic Paul: Gnostic Exegesis of the Pauline Letters* (Philadelphia: Fortress Press, 1975); idem, *The Gnostic Gospels* (New York: Vintage, 1985); and Michael Williams, *Rethinking "Gnosticism": An Argument for Dismantling a Dubious Category* (Princeton NJ: Princeton University Press, 1996) 263-66.

[39]Giovanni Filoramo, *A History of Gnosticism*, trans. Anthony Alcock (Oxford: Basil Blackwell, 1990) xxi.

the origins of America and gnostic thought.[40] He finds that in this "religion-soaked" country, across and beyond the denominations, the gnostic impulse beats strongly in its secret heart. For Bloom, the most characteristic feature of religion in America is the gnostic element: "Gnosticism . . . is now, and always has been the hidden religion of the United States, the American Religion proper."[41]

What is important to note about Bloom's idea is that he does not insist on exact parallels between gnosticism (however it may be defined) and a particular interpretive community. Rather, he acknowledges the hybridizing of American religious groups, and admits the differences between ancient and modern articulations of what might be called gnosticism. He insists on seeing a broad typology that attempts to see gnosticism not as a particular historical movement, but as a type of consciousness, in evidence in ancient and modern world contexts. This allows for a bigger picture of religion, and can be a welcome corrective to a field too often stuck in textual or philological details.

In the aftermath of Heaven's Gate, what emerged was a public, American conversation about the Bible, and other "issues of common cultural concern." As an interpretive community, Heaven's Gate needed to be addressed, for the movement and its radical response had struck a deeply resonant chord with the American public. Yet mainstream ecclesiastical and academic methods of Bible study generally failed to account for such a radical movement and its radical orientation. Mabee's "American biblical hermeneutics" models a useful approach. His insistence on addressing the particularities of different American settings in which communities interact with the text fosters a broader, deeper interaction of Bible and broad cultural concerns. In his exploration of an American religion, Bloom finds himself to be "a Gnostic without hope."[42] Paradoxically, this statement can in one respect also be viewed as hopeful, because it reflects part of the agenda that Mabee sets forth for a public hermeneutic—it "transcends

---

[40]Harold Bloom, *The American Religion. The Emergence of the Post-Christian Nation* (New York: Simon & Schuster, 1992) 30-31.

[41]Ibid., 50.

[42]Ibid., 257.

sacred/secular barriers by incorporating both realms" and in it the "dominant intellectual currents peculiar to the culture become significantly enriched through the critical process."[43] The very exploration of an American biblical hermeneutics that can take into consideration a Harold Bloom and other culture critics as American interpreters of the Bible can inspire hope, insofar as biblical interpretation can be named as an attempt to fathom the "dominant intellectual" and other "currents peculiar to the culture."

---

[43]Mabee, *Reading Sacred Texts*, 121.

Coda

American Biblical Hermeneutics

Personal Observations on the Liquification of Biblical Studies

Charles Mabee

Adventures in Left Field, or Not Being Afraid of the Dark

The reading of the Bible in the American cultural setting is necessarily understood against the background of a more generalized understanding of the role and function of religion within the broader context of society. In this short, personal essay, I wish to make a modest contribution to the essays that Vincent Wimbush has collected around this subject and to move this particular discussion forward imaginatively.

Imagination is the crucial tool at our disposal, not because the facts of the matter are no longer readily at hand, but because facticity is not the issue. Imagination is creative thinking that does not require comprehensive substantiation. It is uncensored. It is not deductive or scientifically based and has questionable value in a rationalistic, pragmatic universe such as the one that dominates in America. It is true that the utilization of imagination makes one particularly vulnerable to criticism. "How do you know that?" "What are your sources?" "What is your legitimation?" My answer is that it feels right based on the theological issues that have been paramount in my mind over the last thirty-five years, and I do not shrink from the fact that American biblical hermeneutics still remains more a matter of art than science.

Our whole training in science-based curriculums of study in our day always intends to manage the imagination in one way or another. Otherwise, where dwells the authority of the professor? The authoritative voice says, "Here are the limits and boundaries of your imagination. Do not transgress them, else you go beyond the reach of evaluation." And, as the light of evaluation fades, then so too does the role of the chosen or appointed authority. Without such evaluation, the dominant culture perishes because the stratification system crumbles. Life is arbitrary and binary. We simply must be able to say such things as yes/no, legitimate/illegitimate, in/out, valid/invalid, and the like. Boundaries and structures must exist and be maintained for us to live. Better to live in a fascistic culture than none at all. Yet, it is precisely the imagination that nurtures and feeds culture. If we program it out at the inception of our discussion, symbolically we have moved the venue of our work from the marriage ceremony to the morgue. The Bible becomes a dead book, and perhaps our culture a dead culture as well.

I want to call attention to one additional point. I am convinced that we in the academic world are too tied to the style of our writing—to our professional genres. An academic essay is meant to be a highly structured argument with supporting statements directed toward the establishment of the major point(s) the essay wishes to make. This genre doesn't accommodate subjective impression very well. Here precision and exactitude are prized as the most valued operations of the mind. In the last analysis, is this not a return to the issue of legitimation and power? There is, in fact, little intrinsically better about more precise ways of thinking over more imaginative ones. Both take brainpower, both are necessary for the continuance of the existence of the species. And that, finally, is what it is all about. Increasingly, that is the point for me. If any of us could choose to be wrong in our intellectual formulations and the culture survive, then we would do so without a moment's hesitation. Surviving, prospering, and enrichment of the species is the task for all of us, not simply for American biblical hermeneuticians.

When I wrote *Reimagining America* some fifteen years ago, I had no ready method at hand for relating the Bible to American culture. I had only my imagination—an imagination that had ironically been nursed in turn primarily by the German theological imagination. Many of my teachers in life have been German—both in the face-to-face manifestation as well as in books. I now know the debt that I owe the Germans for the way I think about theology and America, the two intellectual loves of my life. This debt has become clearer and clearer to me during the course of my teaching career in this very un-Germanic place. Maybe I've just had too many American students ask me, "What are you talking about?"—or, maybe too many colleagues! Certainly, I recall the comment made to me by a friend about the time that *Reimagininag America* came out: "If you want to do American religion, why don't you do American religion." I knew in my soul, I didn't want to "do American religion." I just wasn't interested enough in the subject. I did not feel called to study the history of the American church. (A road not taken, and that has made all the difference.)

It took me a long time before I found out the reason why I didn't want to "do American religion" professionally. And, expectantly or unexpectantly, the answer came from left field while I was teaching yet another introductory course in religious studies at a state university. I found the answer in the teachings of Lao-tzu in his classic text, the *Tao-te Ching*. I found a kindred spirit in Lao-tzu. Lao-tzu laid out a kind of methodology of life in what I would call perpendicular thinking. In its simplest form it goes something like this: If you want to achieve A, then begin with B. Why so? Not to be coy or obscure. But to prepare fertile ground in which something new and imaginative might grow. Lao-tzu believed that darkness not only precedes light, but *must* precede it. Today we might say it differently: "Darkness is not only part of the problem, it is part of the solution." I have come to treasure not only the light, but the darkness as well. I have come to believe that darkness is necessary for the birth of light. If I were a Taoist, I would believe that darkness itself gives birth to the light. On that subject I will remain an agnostic, but the methodological point is well-taken.

I think that another aspect of perpendicular thinking is that you need to build a foundation for yourself outside the thing which you study in order to frame it in a way that will enable it to manifest itself to you in new and imaginative ways. That is, in essence, the method I have used in the exploration of American biblical hermeneutics. In short, I didn't want to be lost in the forest of American religion as I studied the use of the Bible in this particular cultural context. I wanted a different vantage point. A new perspective from which familiar truths were no longer familiar. That is why I termed the enterprise American biblical hermeneutics, rather than the history of American biblical interpretation. I learned that lesson in imagination more from the Germans—somewhere along the line—than from Americans.

It is axiomatic that one learns one's own culture best while living (either literally or figuratively) in the midst of another. The thought of Lao-tzu has helped me understand why. Nonbeing must exist before being. Passivity exists before activity. The stately permanence of the stone exists before the plasticity of water laughingly wears it away into nothingness. (Are stones the traditional compositions of theological thought and water the power of imagination?)

So I began the critical study of the Bible in graduate school with a different sort of agenda and have been at it more or less continuously ever since in various institutions of "higher learning." I have found, unfortunately, that the bulk of my students over the years have had too much of their own powers of imagination stripped from them by the various educational institutions that have shaped them in their own careers. Whatever questions they may have once had about the meaning of life and religion, have all too thoroughly been wiped out and far more mundane concerns have taken up residence in their minds. As far as biblical studies is concerned, the Bible as a book intended to inspire us has all too often been replaced by a model of the Bible that is overly objective. The important thing in this paradigm is content, rather than shaping a way of thinking. I have wanted to imagine the Bible as doing the same thing in my culture as it had done in the cultures that generated it. I was more interested in learning what the Bible *might do* than in what it *had done.*

In final analysis, it was not the historical consciousness of the Germans (especially in the form of historical criticism of the Bible) that had inspired me as much as their imagination that had given rise to that historical consciousness. I am not sure where it was on my journey that I came to the conviction that Germanic historical consciousness itself was a product of the imagination, but I certainly did. And most of my American colleagues in biblical studies seemed to be acting like "history" as an intellectual category was something objective and tangible! Of course, it did give them a specialized form of knowledge which, handled correctly, could lead to promotion and tenure. And that was very tangible and factual, even if "history" itself was far more nebulous and intangible. I found that the genius of the modern German mind was what might be called the "liquification" of intellectual categories. "History" as an intellectual category was just one example of that process of "liquification," in this case liquifying the absoluteness of ecclesiastical control of biblical interpretation. The power of imagination lies in its ability to turn ultimate things into penultimate things. It is the power to stretch out beyond known categories. The Germans had accomplished this task very well. It is a debt that all theologians owe them.

When I wrote *Reimagining America*, I had several overriding convictions. I was certain the Bible had something unique to say to my culture in my time and place. I was certain there were many things about the meaning of the Bible that we hadn't yet discovered, in spite of the immense amount of scholarship that had gone into its study. And, I was certain I didn't want it to be a book about American biblical hermeneutics in the sense of description. I wanted it to inspire others to begin the imaginative task of reading the Bible while taking their own cultural context seriously. Even if I had the ability (which I didn't), I didn't want to *do* American biblical hermeneutics for my readers. I wanted to frustrate as well as inspire in the hope that that frustration would lead them to take the subject seriously. Even though I hadn't studied the mind of Lao-tzu at that stage of my life, I now know I wanted darkness as much as light. Not a frightening, unknowing sort of darkness. But a knowing darkness in which the light might be born. This last point was especially important to me then, as it is now.

Again, the crucial point here is not to do American biblical hermeneutics correctly, but, far more modestly, simply to do it. American biblical hermeneutics is far more a way of being Christian (even as it redefines what being a Christian means), than it is an establishment of definitive categories and perspectives. Thus, I tried to write a book that would not contain the answers so much as it would act as a mirror: "I see something of myself here," or "This makes sense in light of my experience there," and the like were the sorts of responses I wanted to elicit from my colleagues. Only by approaching the subject matter in this way could they be inspired to develop American biblical hermeneutics in their own ways. The book you hold before you is a testimony that not every one in America is afraid of the dark.

Religion, the Child of the Text

In one sense, religion is a complicated business. Without worrying about the myriad of concepts it provides the enquirer, we would do well to inquire into the questions for which these concepts provide an answer. For example, does religion intend to tell us where we as human beings came from and whither we are going? Does it explain the origin and cause of the universe? Does it tell us the nature of the "otherworld," sometimes referred to as the "divine" or "heavenly" realm? Only to the unimaginative eye. While such perspectives are the stuff or vocabulary of religion, by and large they swim on its surface. They don't exist at the level of the deep structure of things which give birth to the deeper matters of the religious impulse. If we choose to look at American biblical hermeneutics with the surface questions of religion in mind, we will quickly run out gas and our journey will be short-lived indeed, and we will soon find ourselves looking elsewhere for guidance in life. For better or worse, American biblical hermeneutics can tell us very little about the nature of God, humanity, or the world itself.

I want to carefully delineate the term "religion" and utilize it in this essay in a very specific way. Handbooks abound which explore it etymologically, and such is not our purpose here. Suffice it to say that the term is associated with Western culture whose "religious" ideas have been framed most profoundly by the Bible. Although not a biblical word per se, it is the biblical consciousness that gives the word its peculiar hue and tone, and I believe it is quite useful to maintain the term in this way and to contrast it with expressions of the primitive sacred that precede it historically. And this means, above all, the eventual association of the term with the written text, most importantly the Bible and the Qur'an. This is simply how we think about religion in the West. As we shop around the world for other religious expressions we immediately inquire as to their texts. If texts are not present in their collective lives, they are something less than authentic religion and more expressions of some sort of primitivism. The great Western religions of Judaism, Christianity, and Islam ultimately justify their existence on the basis of authoritative texts, and we Westerns really can't imagine it being done meaningfully in any other way. Texts legitimate religious communities. The movement from "cult" to "religion" is the movement primarily to texts legitimized by the broader society.

Seen from this perspective, religion becomes a much more simple business. It is fundamentally about the formation of an imaginative, alternative community established by authoritative texts (the "canon"). The religious community functions as an imaginative alternative to the world in which the believers actually live. Therefore, curiosities and claims about the nature of the divine, human, and cosmological realities in which we do in fact live and with which religion does in fact typically traffic, are really the domain of the child . . . and of philosophy. They are not the fundament concerns of religion.

Because religion necessarily traffics in the imagination, it has the problems we can easily associate with the imagination. Legitimacy is the biggest problem of all. The society that does in fact exist, and which religion wishes to supplant, has the authority of the king, or any of the more recent authority institutions which have ameliorated the power of the king (such as presidents, parliaments, prime ministers). Kings have the military to back them up. More importantly, they have priests. Of course, priests traffic in the world of the sacred—but ultimately it is the world of the primitive-sacred that does not yet possess legitimated canonical texts that project an alternative to the world of lived experience. Here I take "primitive" to be roughly synonymous with "pre-canonical"—both of which are ways of describing the world of the priest. In this world the general society "invests" the priest to mediate between the people and the sacred by negotiating the questions of the child which have become the concerns of the adult. Priests provide the professional expertise that deabsolutizes the overriding mood of anxiety that is born from the unanswered philosophical questions of the child. They do this in the service of the "king." The king is the source of all their power and authority. And the king lives off the expertise which the priests bring to bear. Priests are realists, even as they deal with symbols. They are realist because they confront the very real anxieties and meaninglessness of adult life with professional answers and techniques.

From my perspective, these general observations set the stage for the study of American biblical hermeneutics, an example of which you have in your hand. By linking the term "religion" with the rise of a consciousness of the centrality of "authoritative text" (canon), I set the stage for incorporating a new thread into the mixture of strands that compose the religious rope: the strand of "ethical imperative." In order to understand the function of religion and its chief manifestation in canonical text, it is necessary to understand the role which "moral boundary" plays in the whole operation.

In simple terms, the canonical text, and the authentically "religious community" only becomes possible when the desire for moral boundaries of a society become clearly established. Boundaries exist in the context of primitive sacred societies also, but they are hardly moral boundaries. They are boundaries established primarily on the basis of blood, especially as they are established on the basis of kinship and the utilization of violence in both its threatened and actualized forms. Moral boundaries are preeminently textual boundaries.

The single point that unites American society and biblical culture most profoundly as I see it is that both function as societies consciously formulated as linguistic events, that is, as cultures that are established on the basis of moral boundaries rather than blood.

The Bible grows out of the experience of ancient Israel in exile in Babylon. It is an imaginative, literary construction of society, given the possibility of the return from exile to the Promised Land. It represents a second chance crafted by those who would renew the society after the failure of the initial colonization of the land.

America, too, is a linguistic event. Unlike traditional culture, and like the Bible, it does not purport to be so much a description of a place as a process of the human mind. "America" is as much about imaginative social location and relations, as it is about physical spatial location. America provides an answer to the question, "What would happen if you could purposefully, rationally construct a society out of whole cloth?" This purposeful (re)construction of society is a primary commonality between the textual achievement of the ancient Jews and modern America. This is a provocative and legitimate correlation between them that still needs more exploration. Here the text as the sine qua non of religious culture replaces the scapegoating and kinship features of the traditional social order with words, that is, with the mind. Any social order tends to crystallize into hierarchical patterns. While traditional society is grounded in blood, the prophets of ancient Israel rejected the claims of royal autonomy and imaginatively projected a new kind of society in which all citizens shared in the benevolences of the social order regardless of kinship and the power of violence/sacrifice. This new kind of social order represented a fundamental shift of ethics to the primary place in the formation of cultural boundaries.

The new, imaginative prophetic social order that Judaism projected placed the marginal and invisible members of the society at the imaginative center of social, economic, and political life. They became the means by which the entire society was measured and legitimized. They became, in effect, the new imaginative center of society. The result was a revolution in social understanding. It meant, in theoretical terms, the prioritizing of ethics over religion. Rather than the priest being the center of the social order, it was now the "orphan, widow, and stranger." In this reconceptualization of society, the new role of the priest was to serve the marginalized, rather than God. Now religion becomes what it really is, the domestification of the primitive sacred that is pretextual, pre-canonical. In religion it became evident that God could only be known through such service—a lesson hard learned during the course of the Jewish exile in Babylon.

Parallels to the American experience are clear and evident. Whatever claims America has to universality and centrality in the human experience—and it is clear that such claims are frequently made—those claims are based on the prerogative of democracy over other forms of political/social arrangement. Democracy is widely understood to be the means by which the marginalized can find a voice in the affairs of the people. Ideally, democracy is the prophetic spirit systemically embodied in the political order. Furthermore, we may go on to make the claim that to the degree democratic ideals are actualized in American life, the prophetic protection of the marginalized is honored and validated.

But, finally, religion is not political theory. Even democracy cannot usher in either the messianic age or the kingdom of God. Truth is hardly a commodity accessible by democratic voice. The well-being of the minority is not absolutely safeguarded in the principle of rule by the majority. The basic challenge to America by the imaginative biblical faith is this: democracy is no guarantor of the rights of the marginalized. The decisions of even a democratic society can be more injurious to them than the dictates of a benevolent dictator.

Our history teaches us that idolatry in the form of a return of the primitive-sacred was not eliminated by the establishment of textual society, but merely driven underground and reconstituted in more intellectually subtle ways. While America shares the task of myth making for the creation and maintenance of social order with all other cultures, as a textually constructed society it has as profoundly as any other experienced the tracings of the primitive sacred in its social history.

Traditional myth making based on blood is visceral and less tenuous than myth making based on textual identity. It is less fragile because it is reenforced and kept in place by very concrete and powerful markers. These markers are primarily embodied in blood kinship and blood sacrifice (scapegoating) and involve the whole person, including one's emotional, intellectual, economic, and spiritual life. A culture based on text is primarily an intellectual creation that must be constantly nurtured and fed through the intellect since it is grounded linguistically, rather than sacrificially. As the diverse features of human experience come into play, they are fed primarily through the intellect. In this way, the primary danger zone for idolatry in America is in the area of abstracted intellect—a danger that seems to grow each and every year of our existence.

Contributors

Doug Hill continues as a student in the Master of Divinity degree program at Union and also works as a journalist.

Kimberleigh Jordan received the Master of Divinity degree from Union Theological Seminary (New York) in 1997. An ordained minister in the United Church of Christ and a professional dancer, she is currently on the ministerial staff at Marble Collegiate Church, New York City.

Charles Mabee is professor of Old Testament at Ecumenical Theological Seminary, Detroit, and is editor of the Studies in American Biblical Hermeneutics monograph series for Mercer University Press.

Harold Rhee received the Master of Divinity degree from Union Theological Seminary (New York) in 1998. He currently lives and works in Oakland, California.

Rosamond Rodman received the Master of Divinity degree from Union Theological Seminary (New York) in 1997. She is currently in the Ph.D. program in Early Christianity at Columbia University.

David Saul received the Master of Divinity degree from Union Theological Seminary (New York) in 1996. He now does freelance work in computer technology in New York City.

Andrea Smith received the Master of Divinity degree from Union Theological Seminary (New York) in 1997. She is currently in the Ph.D. program in the History of Consciousness at the University of California at Santa Cruz.

Vincent L. Wimbush is professor of New Testament and Christian Origins at Union Theological Seminary (New York), and adjunct professor of Religion, Columbia University, New York City.

Selected Bibliography

Bellah, Robert N. *The Broken Covenant: American Civil Religion in Time of Trial*. New York: Seabury Press, 1975.

Bercovitch, Sacvan. *American Jeremiad*. Madison: University of Wisconsin Press, 1978.

Blonsky, Marshall. *American Mythologies*. New York: Oxford University Press, 1992.

Bloom, Harold. *The American Religion: The Emergence of the Post-Christian Nation*. New York: Simon & Schuster, 1992.

Boone, Kathleen C. *The Bible Tells Them So: The Discourse of Protestant Fundamentalism*. Albany: State University of New York Press, 1989.

Brown, Jerry Wayne. *The Rise of Biblical Criticism in America, 1800–1870: The New England Scholars*. Middletown CT: Wesleyan University Press, 1969.

Cherry, Conrad, editor. *God's New Israel: Religious Interpretations of American Destiny*. Englewood Cliffs NJ: Prentice-Hall, 1971.

Cornelius, Janet D. *"When I Can Read My Title Clear": Literacy, Slavery, and Religion in the Antebellum South*. Columbia: University of South Carolina Press, 1991.

Ellul, Jacques. *The Technological Society*. New York: Alfred A. Knopf, 1967.

Gaustad, Edwin Scott. *A Religious History of America*. New revised edition. San Francisco: HarperSanFrancisco, 1990.

Gunn, Giles, editor. *New World Metaphysics*. New York: Oxford University Press, 1981.

Hatch, Nathan, and Mark Noll, editors. *The Bible in America*. New York: Oxford University Press, 1982.

Jeffrey, David Lyle. *People of the Book: Christian Identity and Literary Culture*. Grand Rapids MI: William B. Eerdmans, 1996.

King, Thomas. *Green Grass, Running Water*. New York: Bantam Books, 1993.

Kort, Wesley. *"Take, Read": Scripture, Textuality, and Cultural Practice*. University Park: Pennsylvania State University Press, 1996.

Lincoln, C. Eric. *Race, Religion, and the Continuing American Dilemma*. New York: Hill and Wang, 1984; revised edition, 1999.

Mabee, Charles. *Reimagining America: A Theological Critique of the American Mythos and Biblical Hermeneutics.* Studies in American Biblical Hermeneutics 1. Macon GA: Mercer University Press, 1985.

_____. *Reading Sacred Texts through American Eyes: Biblical Interpretation as Cultural Critique.* Studies in American Biblical Hermeneutics 7. Macon GA: Mercer University Press, 1991.

Marsden, George M. *Fundamentalism and American Culture: The Shaping of Twentieth Century Evangelicalism, 1870–1925.* London and New York: Oxford University Press, 1980.

Martin, Marty. *Religion and Republic: The American Circumstance.* Boston: Beacon Press, 1987.

Massa, Mark S. *Charles Augustus Briggs and the Crisis of Historical Criticiam.* Harvard Dissertations in Religion. Minneapolis: Fortress Press, 1990.

O'Leary, Stephen D. *Arguing the Apocalypse: A Theory of Millennial Rhetoric.* New York: Oxford University press, 1994.

Ong, Walter J. *Orality and Literacy: The Technologizing of the Word.* London and New York: Routledge, 1982.

Said, Edward. *Orientalism.* New York: Vintage Books, 1978.

Schlesinger, Arthur M., Sr. *A Critical Period in American Religion, 1875–1900.* Philadelphia: Fortress Press, 1967.

Smith, Theophus. *Conjuring Culture: The Biblical Formation of Black America.* New York: Oxford University Press, 1994.

Smith, Wilfred Cantwell. *What Is Scripture? A Comparative Approach.* Minneapolis: Fortress Press, 1993.

Stern, P. V. D. *The Life and Writings of Abraham Lincoln.* New York: Modern Library, 1940.

Tabor, James, and Eugene V. Gallagher. *Why Waco? Cults and the Battle for Religious Freedom in America.* Berkeley: University of California Press, 1995.

Wright, Stuart A., editor. *Armageddon in Waco: Critical Perspectives on the Branch Davidian Conflict.* Chicago: University of Chicago Press, 1995.

Wuthnow, Robert. *The Restructuring of American Religion: Society and Faith since World War II.* Princeton NJ: Princeton University Press, 1988.

Indexes

Name Index

Subject Index

The Bible and the American Myth.
A Symposium on the Bible and Construcitons of Meaning.
    edited by Vincent L. Wimbush
Studies in American Biblical Hermeneutics 16 (StABH 16).

Mercer University Press, Macon, Georgia 31210-3960.
Isbn 0-86554-650-9. Catalog and warehouse pick number: MUP/P193
Text design, composition, and layout by Edmon L. Rowell, Jr.
Camera-ready pages composed on a Gateway 2000 and an AOpen BG45-AP5VM
    via WordPerfect 5.1/5.2 (dos) and WpWin 5.2 (with 6.1 and 7.0.1.9 on-line)
        and printed on a LaserMaster 1000.
Text font: (Adobe) Palatino 11/13 and 10/12.
Display font: (Adobe) Palatino 24-, 12-, and 11-point bf.
Printed and bound by McNaughton & Gunn Inc., Saline MI 48176.
    Printed via offset lithography on 50# Writers Natural (500ppi).
    Perfectbound in 10-pt. cls stock,
        printed one color, and lay-flat laminated.

[May 1999]

043099elr